Socioeconomic And Philosophical Observations

OrangeBooks Publication

1st Floor, Rajhans Arcade, Mall Road, Kohka, Bhilai, Chhattisgarh 490020

Website: **www.orangebooks.in**

© Copyright, 2024, Author

No rights reserved. Any part of this book may be reproduced, stored in a retrieval system, or transmitted, in any form by any means, electronic, mechanical, magnetic, optical, chemical, manual, photocopying, recording or otherwise, without the prior written consent of its writer.

First Edition, 2024

ISBN: 978-93-6554-436-7

SOCIOECONOMIC AND PHILOSOPHICAL OBSERVATIONS

KESHAV SADASHIV SAPRU

OrangeBooks Publication
www.orangebooks.in

Contents

1. Abortion: Paradox In Theory And Practice 1
2. A Completion of Aviation Safety 19
3. A Specific Synthesis Of Religion And Science 37
4. Bringing New Emotions To Nude Art 42
5. Can "Fascist Socialism" Exist? 46
6. Capitalism And Free Money Are Compatible 54
7. Davos Is The Illuminati 58
8. German Querfrot Inspired Radical Fascist Flag 60
9. How Aliens Get Here To Earth 63
10. How To Be A Popular Rightist In A Liberal Democracy. 75
11. How To Make Central Planning Work 91
12. How To Make Science Better 101
13. How To Troll Daesh 104
14. Is Clothing Immoral? 105
15. Marriage Is A Racket 106
16. On The Importance Of Original Meaning In Politics ... 109
17. Paradoxes In Capitalism: Choice And Efficiency 112

18. Paradoxes In Communism:Revolution 116
19. Paradoxes In Conservatism:History 122
20. Paradoxes In Ideology: A Matter of Nature And Purpose 128
21. Paradoxes In Liberalism: Age of Legal Sex 130
22. Paradoxes In Pornography And Hard Drugs: Consumer Degradation 133
23. Paradoxes In Fascism: Strength 136
24. Poverty Has An Endgame 138
25. Reducing Fire Danger In Nuclear Power Plants 142
26. Seeing Can Be Believing 145
27. Socialism Does Everything Better Than Capitalism, Even, Slavery 149
28. The Future Is Scientifically Racist 152
29. The Malmstrom Effect 155
30. Article Begins — 162
31. The Airforce Launches An Investigation 164
32. The Speculation Begins 166
33. Why I Am A Conservative Socialist 176

Socioeconomic And Philosophical Observations

Abortion: Paradox In Theory And Practice

---·◇·---

For those who partake and engage in abortion, it represents their eventual denouement

Black and White Umbrella on White Wall by CappedX, Barundi, Punjab, India, Pexels.com

Fact Based Opinion And Analysis

In much the same vein as the paradox of tolerance that Karl Popper noticed about an internally consistent Liberalism, where he noticed that tolerance of intolerant views would eventually lead to their victory over Liberalism and Liberals in a society, which he advocated for guarding against, it is a similar paradox that we will examine today. It is not necessary for you to agree with this, or even acknowledge its existence, many find the idea that such a central tenent of Liberal thought can undermine it, but perhaps the discomfort therein will show how important it is. Before we move on to the abortion paradox as I see it, the paradox of tolerance can be exapanded in a way that Karl Popper may or may not find less sinister, that being that by believing less and less in the idea of progress, another important aspect of Liberalism, the West is unwittingly causing its own stagnation and demise. Whether this is present only in the English West, or the non-US English West (since the US has more freethinkers due to its strong free speech laws), remains to be seen.

This paradox represents many remarkabilities, they shall be listed and explained as follows:

Remarkabilities In Abortion: Theory And Practice

THE STRIKING SIMILARITY OF OUTCOMES BETWEEN LIBERALISM AND NAZISM WHEN IT COMES TO THE DISABLED

My first point of remarkability comes from the sharp distinction that Liberals and Nazis make between themselves, however, in the Netherlands, the Dutch with pre-natal testing are now able to abort 95% of the foetuses who have the genetic markers for Down Syndrome.

My question is that, is it objectionable only when the methods to remove a group from society is through overt, dramatic and state-led methods such as genocide and mass murder versus from below through individual choices and covert methods such as abortion?

I'm not making a link between Liberalism and Nazism, however in this case, the means are different, but the outcomes (ends) are the same, the destruction of a group of people. And we mustn't forget that the Nazis were after the disabled too. Which is what those with DS are classified as.

I have conducted polls on Reddit on this issue, the supermajority of the voters are in the West.

1. https://www.reddit.com/r/WhatsMyIdeology/comments/1 54jxuw/discussion_poll_nazis_wanted_to_ext erminate_the/? utm_content=title&utm_medium=post_embed&utm_nam e=1527e6c3e70543edad6a4d870d5ffb81&ut m_source=embedly&utm_term=154jxuw

2. https://www.reddit.com/r/IdeologyPolls/comments/154jz7 7/nazis_wanted_to_exterminate_the_disabled_in/?utm_co ntent=title&utm_medium=post_embed&utm_name=1e85 d7c0ec7f4e73a08fd8fad43b8402&ut m_source=embedly&utm_term=154jz77

Regardless Of Ideology Abortion Is A Paradox For Those Who Practice It, But Mostly So For Liberals And Their Offshoots As They Are The Most Committed To It

My second point of remarkability comes from the fact that abortion, much like the paradox of tolerance, represents an issue not just for Liberals, but for those Conservatives who support abortion (population control vs individual choice) and Leftists.

And those are those who will loose the most to ultra-traditionalists and traditionalists, who have a multitude of children, anywhere from 6 to 13, if they remain unrepressed.

As the population of the ultra-traditional and traditional increase in countries which don't repress such peoples (example of repression People's Republic of China, North Korea, etc.), the populations of those who support abortion for a variety of reasons [individual choice, population control, personhood starts after birth or adult rituals (where infanticide can also be justified, although this is not a pre-requisite, as other societies like India also used to have a well-observed practice of infanticide in regions)], will fall gradually over time (in the World this could be from 1–300 years), while those who have a lot of children, may be small in number but would eventually come to make up the largest proportion of population in the country.

This is visible in a fast pace (in demographic terms) in Israel, where the Haredim used to make up a small proportion of the population of Israel in 1949, about 3.5%, but now roughly make up about 13.5% of the population of Israel, and by 2050 would be about 24%. They had 7.5–8.5 TFR (Total Fertility Ratio, that is the total number of children a woman has through her lifetime), and now have 6.5–7.5 TFR, while Conservative Jews have a TFR of 3, the Liberal and Reformist Jews have about 2.

I should point out that this excoriates those who are ideologically distinct from Liberalism as well, but also carry out abortions for reasons of their own (even if their intentions are internally well-meaning), as mentioned earlier, this can include the Conservatives (population control stemming from the pessimism of Malthusian/Erlichian collapse and controlling the perceived uncontrolled breeding of the poor), the Left (emancipation of women from motherly duties and house chores, never mind the chores and duties they have to fulfill of Socialism and Communism or any other ideology, hmmm...? In the guise of freedom, women continue to do the very duties which they did in Victorian times, except now it is for themselves and no one else, those who take care of others children have the entire package of Victorian duties, except now they do it for themselves, production and consumption don't stop, you can merely change the relations therein), etc.

And Victorian Values also promoted Pro-Natalism, people had large families in cities and larger ones in the countryside, they were paid less, but things were also cheaper, one could say that there was less to spend on, but the poor today also spend less. Many of the modern conveniences of today existed in '50s and '60s, yet people had large families, or atleast larger than today, so, I view the economic argument with skepticism and unconvincing and more as largely as an excuse to not have children.

For example, in my observations, the Senseito Party, a party considered more to the right of the long- reelected Liberal Democratic Party of Japan has won the seat of Okinawa Prefecture from them, OP has the highest birth rate in the entirety of Japan.

Correlation is not causation, but it makes you think doesn't it? :D To see this trend out into the future:

The UN Population Study for the year 2300 (made in the year 2002) has many ranges for population in the year 2300, the lowest population projections would be for the lowest birth rates, high education in women, widespread contraception, small family sizes, etc. While not in the study, higher abortion levels, suppression of religion and birth abstinence would likely lead to lower population than the lowest range in this study. It's important to point out that the Haredi work, but women work more. They work quite a bit in the IT industry, so work and education in women, shouldn't be taken as a force which uniformly reduces birth rates, although it does in most cases and groups of women. Haredi men work, but at lower rates than the women, because they have to study the old religious texts, supported by government subsidy and are not conscripted (one could say their job is to preserve living heritage versus museum heritage).

Although a small contingent of 1500 Haredi Battlion exists, which allegedly the government wants to increase by 100%, leading to intense protests.

Additionally, a pretty up-to-date study by the Lancet, shows that widespread contraception and female education would lead to their lowest range by 2100 (which is pretty low), even so, following current trends (extrapolated) would lead to about 8.3–8.6 billion by 2100, which is lower than UN projections, even if they are from 2022 (their study shows 10.4 billion).

For other religious or ultra-religious groups which are measured:

The Amish Birth rate is pretty high, but it depends on the external economy which they trade with, but those birth rates don't fall below the replacement rate or even get close to it.

US Pentecostals and non-denominational Christians among others to have 2.4 birth rate.

And the presumed African Century from growth, however, African birth rates in most sub-saharan countries are also close to replacement when infant and child mortality is considered (I cannot locate this study), even without that study, I have studies which show the persistence and uneven transition to replacement fertility and the conflict with large family sizes and high fertility, pro-natalism and low family planning versus unmet contraception needs in women (the conflict can be in women too, who may want large families but also want contraception) and the other study covers the high mortality in under-5s and at the other end of the age bracket (cross-pressured mortality rates).

My polls related to this are:

(Votes are cast by forums with a supermajority of those in the West):

1. [POLL] A pro-abortion stance is a logical paradox for liberals in the long run. : r/IdeologyPolls (reddit.com)
2. [Poll] [Discussion] A pro-abortion stance is a logical paradox for liberals in the long run. : r/WhatsMyIdeology (reddit.com)

My third point of remarkability while it only has one data point that I'm aware of and is publicly available on a wide number of sources, is that those who have a large number of children, regardless of their ideology, but as shown earlier, are likely to be more conservative than average or some variant of traditional or ultra-traditional, would see the largest number of LGBT+ people born to them, imagine that, those who are "pro-life" would have the most number of the group of people that western progressives are currently championing for at this moment. If we assume that Western Progressives are correct and that being LGBT+ is more about biology than society (maybe to establish these as essential traits to them, which I also find ironical, since they argue against essentialism when it comes to "cisheteronormativity", or that the normal baseline is normal and essential in the West, but that's an observation for another time) then those that have the most children and those who are in support of having the most children, would also have the most LGBT+ children potentially.

This is 1 out of the 11 children that Elon Musk has had, which brings us to just under 10% of the children which he has had, who is non-conforming (to use a more neutral and less politically charged term). To extrapolate this to the largest cohort of children that individuals can have, whether the more common upper-bound of 13, or even enormous number of offspring of 24, 45, 64, 77, etc. this would correspond to atleast 1 non-conforming child among those who reproduce prolifically, and at most 8, when one looks at the highest bounds, yes, Liberals and their offshoots may inculcate non-conformity in their children, but judging by the number of children that most Liberals have, it's likely to be max 2 by cultural values. Those who have a lot of children, may also increase the probabiltiy of more non- conforming children on purely biological terms, so they could theoretically beat the max amount for the Liberals. Some may counter that these children will suffer under the traditionalists, that might be true for some, but these well. It's also likely, that were it not for contraceptives, more individuals would be born, who could have the biological and the cultural traits of large families. The biological trait is superfecundity and low harmful mutations in the genome and the cultural trait is a preference for large families and to be exceedingly pro-life (even if say that in the city, those who want 13 children may not have the said 13, that they could in the countryside, they would likely still have a lot of children, as reported from Niger).

My Fourth Point of Remarkability (axiomatic) those capitalists and socialists who support abortion, are merely reducing their own future consumers, manufacturers, producers, workers, administrators, etc. leading potentially to their inexorable self-extinction (productivity increases are not infinite or indefinite, and eventually, a declining population will lead to falls in economic output).

My Fifth Point of Remarkability (axiomatic) that for those feminists who describe the Foetus in unflattering terms such as "parasite", it takes little to remind them that the Foetus protects the mother against environmental pollution in the environment, as both bodies serve to filter pollutants in the environment from each other's bodies, acting in tandem. This is more total, when it comes to radiation, than any other pollutant, whereas the Foetus absorbs the most radiation, protecting the mother from harm, as nascent and growth heavy cells absorb the most amount of radiation than any other cell in the body, save for stem cells. When it comes to physical assault, mothers have a greater chance of survival, as awful as it sounds, because the Foetus acts as a barrier to physical trauma. Life in its many forms and shapes shows that the relations between individuals is not simple, but complex, if we are to look at the benefits and burdens of pregnancy, then it is important to get a full picture, as mainstream utilitarianism does not balance every pro or every con, as those require complex analysis and weighing many different facts and their relation to each other. Even if we look at it in purely scientific terms, nothing about the Foetus implies an overwhelming burden or weight on the mother, all organisms rely on each other, without which life would be impossible on our planet, regardless of the nature of that reliance. Weak appeals to science, without looking at the entire breadth and depth of scientific thought are unhelpful, especially in such complex cases. Scientific, moral, religious and so on, can all justify preservation of the foetus, creating a triangulation between secular and unsecular thoughts and systems. Let us not forget that according to biology, once the gametes fuse, new DNA is created and new life comes into existence.

Not to beat a dead horse like a cooky, old and cough-ridden conservative, but I find all these amusingly and highly ironic.

:D

In Closing

Returning to a more serious tone, the point of this entire long text is that those who advocate for abortion the strongest will decline in time to be at unimportant levels, while those who do not support it the strongest, will, if we assume that they are not repressed (this point is to exclude countries where they have been wiped out or are highly diminished or repressed like China, North Korea and Russia, which has seen strong religiosity and traditionalism drop consistently, even if there has been a revival in religiosity in Russia, it is a weak revival, as pew research has shown, those 49%+ christians and theists are weak believers) will be the largest groups to exist in society in the end. If and when this happens, populations and the economies of the World will rebound, but they will be structurally more religious and traditional, without a doubt. They will likely preserve the knowledge and wisdom of the old world, but how they will use it, or whether a new enlightenment is possible in the future, that is, whether these 7–800 years from the 1600s to the 23 or 2400s are emblematic of a cycle of enlightenment and reversal, or merely an aberration in the predominantly religious history of man, remains to be see, I do think that it is the latter, however, maybe the more accurate picture is that in this predominantly religious world of man, rationalism rises up, only to die out, and this near-1000 year period we see before us, is merely a stronger signal, due to the vast economic, political, social and historical forces at work, likely to never be repeated at this scale and intensity ever again. I trust that they will preserve the knowledge, as many earlier gatherers and seekers of knowledge were traditionalists and old-fashioned conservatives and not just in the Western sense of the term.

Those countries which changed their cultural values to be more pro-life like Georgia and Kazakhstan, saw a resurgence in their population levels, may be due to their smaller and more remote status in relation to their big brother, the proportion of the ultra-traditional and religious make up a bigger proportion of their country's in a relative sense, much like Israel, allowing for this strong revival in birth, unlike in Russia, which likely has seriously denuded the old growth-centric populations it had, due to the huge changes that the Soviet Union carried out, even if it became so-to-speak conservative under Stalin.

If Liberals, Conservatives and the Materialist and non or anti-religious Left do not recognize this, it is likely that they will be a very denuded remnant of their old self, a few hundred years in the future, likely by the 25th century or before.

My polls for this on reddit are at the following links (the same advisory as before of a supermajority of the voters being in the West continues):

1. Remarkable Peculiarities In The Theory And Practice Of Abortion : r/IdeologyPolls (reddit.com)

Certainly, there is no guarantee that values among traditionalists outside of large families and birthing have not changed, it could be that unlike my prior statement of faith about the traditional preserving knowledge accumulated, when most other ideological and philosophical adherents have died out or are greatly diminished. And I don't mean the solely sensationalist, erotic, nudity not connected to the divine and other lascivious forms of knowledge, I also mean, information which they may not think preserving, due to its non-theological nature. Now there maybe librarians or pursuers of knowledge, scribes, etc. who may assiduously preserve Old World Information, but its dissemination to the larger society, may not happen. Additionally, even in our current so-to-speak "Liberal Era", research done in countries presumed to be Liberal, do not reach or are read by everyone, they are in expensive journals and even if they were free, would be for the perusal of those interested and have atleast a basic understanding of the concepts being discussed, not something which everyone has.

Intellectual laziness is not a conservative hegemony as oft derided by Liberals. Whether from lack of interest, resources, time, inclination, or any other number of factors that prevent individuals from understanding the issues around them.

My Opinion On The Matter

Judging by the nature of abortion, its contradictions and the potential for cheapening human life (yes along with the many other things in the world, which require their own response), it is a measure that should be reserved for only the most extreme case, that killing the baby will save the mother. As here one life is being balanced against another. We should also advance incubation technology to such an extent that we can grow "dangerous" foetuses independently of the mother. Prioritizing and centralizing the importance of human life in all its forms. Those who have suffered from rape, should be offered either a surrogate home, or a painless removal of the foetus into an advanced incubation chamber, etc. although a 1996 study showed that 38% of the mothers examined in the US kept their baby, or atleast saw it to term after a rape (their religious/ideological beliefs were not listed, another one said 32.2%).

This shows that how even under duress, humans try to avoid sacrificing children, experiences from the famines in the Soviet Union and the People's Republic of China, mothers and fathers called for their children to eat their corpses to survive, those who were forced to eat their own children or bury them alive, saw many of them die soon after from grief. There is no doubt that man loves its children dearly, even in scenarios of hyperstress. There can be so many solutions to the complex problem of abortion that we should be willing to consider all of them. Technology should serve man, and not the other way around.

Let's not become an entry in a cookbook. :D

PS: Of course, what would need to be considered is whether growing children in vats or incubation chambers for very premature children (functionally not different from vats in my view), would lead to a reduction in the value of children, since growth in wombs and breastfeeding leads to an emotional bond between mothers and newborns (among other benefits and developments). Adopting a technology such as this, even if it provides the benefit of nearly abolishing abortion and abortive infanticide as a maladaptive practice from the pre-historic era (that's a big if), it would still create other problems in the form of breaking the bond between mother and child at a stage which is biologically very important for bonding both during and after pregnancy (the method of abortion itself is quite invasive and disruptive, requiring, when the foetus is highly developed to have its head crushed and its body vacuumed out), one would have to consider whether a) This method is less worse than abortion in technological terms which don't affront morality, which I think that it is and b) whether it preserves mother and offspring bonds, hearing the heartbeat and breathing of the still growing foetus in an artificial support chamber should do atleast part of the job. Sharing the dopamine and oxytocin releases from mother and offspring, where the mother here is the foster mother, should also atleast partly mimic the physical bond, although as mentioned earlier, the mutually protective and symbiotic relationship of mother and foetus would still be broken. Inspite of these, I would still think of it as much more preferable to abortion as a method and technology.

And even having said this, the best solution whether organic from increasing proportion of traditionalists in the population, to an engineered solution of greater natalism in society (although I prefer the organic solution), this technology and method is only a stop-gap, till a structural cultural change is made and society is more pro-natal as a whole.

As my polls show that most people and most liberals do not understand this dynamic or reject it outright, indicating how little they understand of their decline in the West, the bastion of Liberalism, and perhaps in India too, where abortion is virtually uncontroversial politically speaking. Both Left, Right, Conservative, Liberal, etc. parties see it as much.

Ceasing migrations to the West will show them their policy fallacies quicker and unrestricted support and access to abortion in India will lead to a similar denouement of all those who have no problem with it. One might say that this is due to the Hindu Rebirth thinking, that all souls are reborn, that "consensual, undiscriminating" abortion is unproblematic in India politically (except for some obscure christian fundamentalist and militant parties in the North-East), but I find this explanation silly and simplistic. Son preference plays a role, but with gender ratios now normalizing as according to NFHS-5 and the decline in sex-selective abortions and infanticide, there doesn't seem to be any sense in the further loosening of abortion restrictions by the Supreme Court and the ruling BJP government, nor any reason or reasons with good and broad explanatory power (of why India finds abortions virtually uncontroversial, atleast in an overt basis outside of our culture specific focus on sex-selective abortion stemming from a now-declining son preference).

Sources

1. https://www.theatlantic.com/magazine/archive/2020/12/the-last-children-of-down-syndrome/ 616928/

2. https://www.timesofisrael.com/nearly-1-in-4-israelis-will-be-ultra-orthodox-by-2050-study-says/

3. https://www.japantimes.co.jp/news/2022/08/08/national/politics-diplomacy/okinawa-sanseito- popularity/

4. http://www.asahi.com/ajw/articles/14836699#:~:text =Okinawa%20Prefecture's%20fertility %20rate%2C%20or,population%20decline%20in%20February%202021

5. https://www.mercatornet.com/islands-of-fertility-in-east-asia-okinawa-and-amazingly-north- korea

6. https://www.scmp.com/week-asia/health-environment/article/3042812/fertility-secrets-okinawa- give-birth-hope-sexless

7. https://www.un.org/development/desa/pd/sites/www.un.org.development.desa.pd/files/files/documents/2020/Jan/un_2002_world_population_to_2300.pdf

8. https://www.thelancet.com/article/S0140-6736(20)30677-2/fulltext

9. wpp2022_summary_of_results.pdf (un.org) [top of page 9 of the PDF, or (ii) of the document]

10. https://www.ncbi.nlm.nih.gov/pmc/articles/PMC8417155/#:~:text=While%20Amish%20mortality%20rates%20dropped,Amish%20woman%20(this link specifically highlights the TFR of 6 to 8, but you can read the rest of the study to get a full understanding as I did)

11. https://ifstudies.org/blog/americas-growing-religious-secular-fertility-divide

12. https://foreignpolicy.com/2022/05/13/africa-century-economic-growth/

13. https://www.ncbi.nlm.nih.gov/pmc/articles/PMC4011385/

14. https://www.thelancet.com/journals/langlo/article/PIIS2214-109X(22)00337-0/fulltext

15. https://www.bbc.com/news/technology-61880709

16. https://archive.ph/2024.03.30-053906/https://www.ft.com/content/838eeb4e-3bff-4693-990f- ff3446cac9b2

17. https://archive.ph/o/DBGQ7/https://www.ft.com/content/e577411e-3bf2-4fb4-872a- 8b7d5e9139d3

18. https://pubmed.ncbi.nlm.nih.gov/8765248/

Socioeconomic And Philosophical Observations

A Completion of Aviation Safety

The time is now to get aviation done

Woman Giving A Presentation, London, England, United Kingdom, The Coach Space, Public Domain, Pexels.com

[Pre-script: after speaking to a pilot who wished to remain anonymous, I got feedback. The conversation between us will follow below, and is paraphrased and rearranged for clarity and emphasis. If the pilot did not mention something in the article, it doesn't necessarily mean that a view does not exist, it may be that the pilot

focused on issues considered more important or which stood out.

Pilot: While favourable to the idea of the article in part, there was a cautionary advice about writing an article about the technical details of planes and improvements to them if not from an aeronautics engineering background (an advice reiterated later on in our conversation, this is pointed out here not to take away from this advice, but to establish it beforehand and make the reader aware, for ease in reading). I took recognition of this warning and expressed thanks at the feedback while expressing hope that this article could help in someway. The pilot pointed out that many of the things mentioned in this article were already covered on technical point, are covered by other systems of present in the aircraft and in general are unfeasible given the nature of the aircraft and how they're used. The pilot went on to say that while my article was researched, the nature of the topic is so vast and requires such breadth that it is conceivable and expected that I missed something, as learning is an ongoing process, much the same for pilots.

Having said that, the pilot goes on to acknowledge an aspect of my article which is pertinent, the human element. Stigma attached to mental health in aviation, bad rosters, long duties, etc.

The pilot mentions that smoke hoods are present in the cockpit besides the oxygen masks, but they're situation specific.

Me: I mention that I meant smoke hoods for the passengers, although I do acknowledge the problem with feasibility with such a solution.

Pilot: The pilot mentions that what is interesting is that there is no central oxygen system (not clarified whether there used to be or there isn't one now), and that each row has its own chemical oxygen generator which can last for 15 mins, which are activated when tugged.

Fire in the cabin is a byproduct of another uncontrollable fire, there are things in place to keep that at bay.

Me: That is something which I had not considered, so a malfunction would happen from some malfunction or mechanical blockage.

Pilot: Yes, and it would be independent to that row.

Pilot shares image of the oxygen masks and a canister connected to them

Short exchange about the fire discussed before (main effort to land plane) and a few unrelated topics

Pilot: The pilot said that we cannot not have wing fuel tanks, because they are essential to the stress relief of the wings and the airframe, they are also the ones which are filled the first with fuel. Modular fuel cells are already a thing. They're called ACTs or Additional Centre Tanks (as per requirements).

[In-between I Harken back to an earlier comment made by me, the topic of why scrubbers are useless, I ask the actions that they take in the case of a fire, descending to a lower altitude, about whether it would reduce cabin

pressure or in the case of an engine fire where the engines could be off. The pilot answers that descent would not lead to a differential pressure (I imagine which would be noticeable), as they descend to 10,000 ft (roughly 3,334 m) the air which is let in is through the ram intake and not the engines]

Pilot: We also have multiple hydraulic redundancies in airliners, things get interesting as we lose the hydraulic lines but are able to land the planes just fine (not asked, not specified by which mechanism).

Pilot (contd...): Also oddly enough it's the airforce and the navy guys who have a harder time landing the plane because the aircraft dynamics, procedures and behaviour is different.

Me: Like a sportscar vs a bus

Pilot: Eventually they also become one with their machine but no captain is released without being able to demonstrate that he can control and land the most broken of planes...Not only that, procedurally, design wise very different...Even between airliners...An A320 and a 737 are poles apart...And yes different companies (airliners) do have different procedures internally as well.

Me: Yes, this is usually done through extensive and regular simulator training?

Pilot: 6 month recurrent checks and type training

[The pilot viewed the ideas of the coverage of the human component and the fuel foam favourably.]

After some concluding remarks about American Airlines Flight 587 in 2001 and its crash due to structural failure brought about by erroneous pilot training program of American Airlines with respect to the section where the pilot spoke about how different procedures (among other things) can be between both planes and airliners.

I thanked the pilot and with acknowledgement by the pilot the interview for this article ended.

――――――――――――――――――――

Opinion Piece Organizational Culture

Many articles have gone into the change in the Organizational Culture of Boeing, so I will not go into painstaking detail. But what I will lay bare is that decentralization in High Reliability Organizations like Nuclear Power Plants and Aircraft Manufacturers among others, is dependent on various approaches. Organizations like Mondragon, Haier, AMUL, Semco, etc. show that market socialism and labour ownership can give workers a vested interest in the success of the enterprise, which perhaps they always did, however it also gives them decision-making power.

But, even if we do not head towards full or partial labour ownership and management, a capital owned enterprise like Alco, can also decentralize decision making to workers, so that they feel involved in the business itself, this leads to decisions which lead to an improvement in the organization's culture, where profit is important, but it is not God, so to speak.

Change The Breathing Masks

Breathing masks in planes, which protect pilots and passengers should be upgraded to very capable smoke hoods. Pilots already have advanced masks which cover pilots' faces, however, if all are upgraded to smoke hoods would provide protection atleast uptil 5 mins, preventing unconsciousness during a fire or decompression, which allows for easier evacuation. If it takes too long to take off the smoke hoods, a button should allow rapid deconstruction of the smoke hood, sort of like a controlled explosion, to allow the users of the smoke hoods to escape easily when it's time for evacuation.

Scrubbers

Like spacecraft, planes should have scrubbers. While modern upholstery, fuselage, etc. are all adapted to have materials like Nomex, carbon fibre, which give off relatively less toxic smoke made up of Carbon Monoxide, Dioxide and the almost completely non-lethal Water Vapour. These scrubbers would soak up the hazardous gases (except water vapour), giving everybody more time till evacuation. This is separate from the normal scrubbers which remove CO2 during normal operation. Emergency Scrubbers would kick in when fires break out. There would also have to be a balance in scrubbing so that the extinguishing properties of CO and CO2 aren't negated, merely to keep their levels sufficiently below suffocation and incapcitation.

Fuel Foam And Modular Fuel Tanks

Nowadays fuel is less combustible and has anti-misting features which allow fires to be less catastrophic and not spread as furiously as they used to do so before. However, we know that during crashes, fuel in the tanks causes large explosions, killing people. While the issue of current jumping from higher voltage to lower voltage which caused fuel vapour explosions in a few planes, due to near empty fuel tanks and heating from below due to heating or cooling systems (dependent on the plane which was involved) has been solved (including when fuel gets too cold).

While there has been improvement in the inflammability of Jet Fuel for commercial liners, adding JP-5 Jet Fuel or better (in terms of the fuel flash point, where higher is better), then it would be an improvement over current levels.

However, a crash can still cause massive explosions is well known and need not be repeated, so, if a plane is suspected to crash, the pilots should have the tools to make the fuel completely inert. The way to do this would be a last ditch option to inject thick, cold and coagulant foam, which turns the fuel into a thick, cold and mushy soup which cannot move, burn or anything else, except just sit there.

This means that if the pilots are sure that the plane is going to crash into land, the fuel cannot explode at all.

Planes which flew into terrain (the ground) which had empty or nearly empty fuel tanks saw many more survivors than those which had plenty of fuel.

The problem with concentrating fuel in large fuel tanks in the middle of the planes (under the passenger cabin) and inside the wings is all too self-evident, such large concentrations of fuel create the huge conflagrations, especially if the plane is large, such as in jumbo jets, upon their crashing. If the fuel foam injectors fail, then the explosions would still happen, so, to prevent this, the breaking up of the fuel tanks into smaller and more spread out fuel tanks, would also help contain the fire. Planes could have a small aerodynamic bulge, either above or below (like the Beluga cargo plane) which could house the extra modular fuel tanks, which may not fit entirely in their conventional positions from earlier (due to their increased numbers), this reorientation of the fuel tanks while maintaining the centre of gravity, would mitigate the danger of fire upon crashing quite substantially, even if the failsafes themselves fail, as it would be a structural redesign. These cordoned off fuel tanks would also be separated from the passenger cabin by a lightweight but armoured bulkhead, to prevent its easy spread. No fuel tank would be too far away from the engines, to prevent their flame out while cycling up or cycling down.

The fuel foam injectors would be in a cordoned off section of their respective fuel tanks, so the pilots could expect almost if not 100% fuel neutralization, if they so choosed too engage them. Their cordoned off sections would open to neutralize the nearby fuel, as the feed from these fuel tanks would be shutoff to prevent damage to the engine from foam particles, this would be a measure if all else failed, as the only way to restart the engines would be if the fuel tanks were cleared. This procedure would also help protect the engines from any malfunctioning fuel foam injectors, so that a misfire does not bring down a plane.

Pilot Suicide: Bring Back The Third Wheel

Now that planes and flying have become so safe, that pilot suicides are the real cause of death above accidents, we must address this highly grave issue.

Earlier, cockpits had two pilots, a navigator, a radioman, an engineer and even possibly a sixth or seventh person, depending on how many deadheads (travelling pilots) they had. If somebody did feel suicidal or tried to suicide the plane, the problem they would face, would be that they would've been ganged up on, or their "mistakes" be corrected by all the other people in the cockpit, making pilot suicide earlier a very low chance of death of passengers. Not to mention that some studies show that neuroticism and mental illness has increased in the World in the past 100+ years.

It would be preferable to have two extra people in the cockpit today, even if it costs more. So, that if one person goes to the toilet, there are atleast 1 or 2 people present to restrain the suicidal individual.

In FedEx flights which had such setups, those which faced a murder-suicide by disgruntled employees, deadhead or otherwise, would see a greater survival rate, as there would be more people to restrain the potential troubled agent.

Those which show signs of suicidal behaviour, patient-therapist confidentiality should be lifted to protect future passengers and such pilots should be given help, or if their suicidal tendencies can't be fixed or require more time, then they should get their severance packages or pensions early, so that they can be safely and comfortably removed without causing problems, the government should cover these expenses, if some privately or publicly traded companies complain about profit margins and investor sentiment, then transition grants, loans or subsidies could be given. All these measures could improve the situation related to suicidal pilots.

To prevent the stealth murder-suicide of the like of MH 370, then those pilots who carry out simulations to fuel exhaustion or rapid descents of greater than 25,000 ft, should have these simulations logged into a server, to determine whether they have any such intent, through non-confrontational questioning.

Greater Hydraulics Redundancy And The Propulsion Controlled Aircraft System

Engine breakoffs, engine destruction, cargo hold explosions, bird strikes, missile strikes, bombs, etc. all cause catastrophic damage in the hydraulics assembly, which can bring down a plane, due to loss of control and very few pilots, perhaps the rare individual among tens of thousands, who can successfully land a plane through engine thrust alone, usually these pilots are Navy or Airforce trained.

The way to prevent this, is to add an extra 1 or 2 hydraulic lines at the base of the plane, whereas most planes have 2–3. To extend this, we should add four hydraulic lines on each side of the plane and on the top, by thickening the fuselage and the wing and adding three to four lines more to the wing, to prevent catastrophic loss of control, if a damage incident cuts the main hydraulic lines and the backups at the base of the plane. This would ensure that having 16+ extra hydraulic lines would prevent a single catastrophic damage causes the plane to be unnavigable. On the other hand, if a series of catastrophic incidences overwhelms all these extensive backups, then a computer system called the Propulsion Controlled Aircraft System can be activated which uses careful, fine and continuous engine thrust manipulation to stabilize the aircraft and bring it down safely to a rest. This computer system has been tested by NASA, then it should be added to all existing commercial airliners.

Decentralizing the hydraulic lines, much like veins and capillaries which extend from the arteries, would in the case of a catastrophe, allow sufficient mitigation in the case of such an event. Not to mention, the importance of safety cutoff valves.

It would have to be considered whether the PCAS could be connected to the speed brakes, as deployment of the speed brakes does reduce the constant rising and falling motion which accompanies hydraulic failure. But early or too late deployment could jeopardize the stricken plane. Perhaps the pilots would know when best to deploy the speed brakes, however the potential hypoxia could degrade their decision making powers at that height.

It might be best, due to the lessons learnt from the MCAS system's prior implementation in Boeing planes, that most or all of the system should be in the control of the pilots, even if their is a danger of pilot degradation from hypoxia.

A final way to protect against "pilot" suicide would be to reinforce the cabin door against .357 magnum rounds, to prevent a forced entry from a concealed weapon that doesn't show up on scanners (homemade weapons specially designed to evade scanning).

Structural Reinforcement

Examining the crashes of planes, would bring to our awareness, which parts of the plane should be reinforced when accounting for survivorship bias. Parts which usually give way under extreme stress, are the tail section, the seats, the wings, the engine emplacements which connect the engine to the wing, the elevators, the ailerons, the rudder, the top part and bottom parts of the fuselage around the bottom middle and the top middle regions of the fuselage and the cargo hold and any other parts which have a tendency to shear off when under extreme stress. So, Titanium should be used to reinforce these sections and and double and thicken the holdings around these sensitive areas.

The overall reduction relative to the 40% composites now found in planes (without removing the composites, but by adding the Titanium) would also increase the resistance to lightning found in the thunderstorms like older planes.

Sensor Backup

Rarely what happens in planes is that some ground crew can cover the sensors and forget to remove them during the cleaning process, this can lead to crashes, when the computers on the plane get bad data and blind the pilots through noise and uncertainty.

Emergency Backup Sensors with popout covers could give a backup to the main sensors now covered, preventing a catastrophic accident.

In addition to this it would be advisable to add to many planes the rudimentary lasers that allow for a basic altitude data by a simple narrow beam that goes down and then is reflected back up to the plane, giving the said basic reading, which would atleast give the pilots some basic information, so that they would not hit terrain, reducing one problem, in the case of sensor failure.

Digital sensors have a propensity to fail, although rare, giving the autopilot bad data, turning the AP off does help the pilots to regain control of the craft (this holds true as MCAS is no longer resistant to disabling, hopefully), but now without properly functioning digital instruments, pilots are flying blind and can rely only on their experience and senses, which can be unreliable if it is dark outside and if there's no reference on the ground, due to no lights or if the ground turns to water.

But if there are backup analog controls, then what it means is that in the failure of the digital systems, the pilots atleast have something to help them. This could also hold true if the analog systems fail, then the digital can be there as a backup.

To adjust for the potential clutter and overload of information by having both digital and analog sensors, the digital displays could be selected to read the analog data and reflect it, which would make it a hybrid system, electromechanical.

Countermeasures And Evasive Maneuvers And Electronic Warfare

There are times when commercial planes are shot at, while I am not advocating for very complex, military grade countermeasures, what I would advocate for are at the very least chaff and flares, to give commercial airliners a fighting chance against hostile missiles fired against the plane. It would also be important to have basic jamming equipment (infrared, dazzlers, etc.), so that the RADARs onboard could give the planes a fighting chance against said missiles and provide advanced warning when they're locked on by missiles and the prior recommendations for structural reinforcement would also allow for some evasive measures, without overstressing the plane's structure.

Enhancing Crew Resource Management And Training

In societies that value hierarchy and the authority of a single man or person (male-centric societies can also show similar deference if a woman is in power, especially if backed by elite males), then overreliance on the influence of one person or of hierarchy in general, can be dangerous if different viewpoints can't be expressed, which might save lives and the plane. Egypt Air Flight 990 is one such example, where the First Officer Al Batouty received much respect and deference, beyond his right and his behaviour warranted. Even if we assume for one moment, he did not do a murder-suicide (unlikely, but for the sake of argument), even then, he should not have had so much influence to get into the cockpit before his time, and unnecessarily encouraged to do so. However, no one could've anticipated his precipitous actions, if his past rustication from Egypt Air was unknown.

It may be that even in individualist societies or more egalitarian societies, those individuals who have depth of persona and intense charisma may ride roughshod over opposition to their actions, separate from the appropriate deference that a Captain is due in that environment and in those circumstances.

It would also, finally, be important to carry out training of rare incidents, like losing the hydraulic pressure, or going into a microburst, or not cross-feeding fuel into a leaking fuel tank (when the warnings are anomalous, low oil pressure, high oil temperature and so on), unless there is a need to keep the engines going due to loss of hydraulic pressure.

Lidar

LASER Direction and Ranging would allow aircraft to view Clear Air Turbulence and Microbursts, which RADAR cannot view, as light diffraction and refraction from the clear air would allow the aircraft to view potential dangerous changes of wind and pressure in clear weather, which the RADAR cannot pick up or regions of particularly dangerous weather invisible to RADAR in large storms like Mesocyclones.

Biodynamic Body And Wings With In-Body Engines

A biodynamic design for body and wings, with in-body engines, like the British Comet or the B-2 Spirit Bomber, inspired by birds of prey and their flexibility and sleek aerodynamism, would not only allow for efficient fuel usage and resistance to turbulent weather (and if needed any evasive measures) and better wind flow around these planes, but also allow planes to take off faster behind each other, as their streamlined shapes would allow better resistance to the wing-tip vortices present behind taking off planes. Saving time and money without sacrificing safety.

Training Neutral Bank Angle Indicator

Anglo-American and European bank angle indicators inform the pilot of the bank angle with a subtle but important difference from their former Soviet/Russian counterparts. On the former, the bank angle is indicated by the horizon changing, but the plane remaining stationary, while in the former Soviet/Russian ones it is the plane that changes direction on the indicator and not the horizon. This has lead to crashes and near-misses in the past. Training for former Soviet/Russian pilots is extended by 3 months to compensate for this. However, it would be better to have a neutral bank angle indicator, where the artificial horizon is changed for an equally large display which states the bank angle in the following manner, **L 45°** or **R 45°** (example), which would make it much easier for pilots to understand regardless of their training, as long as they know basic english.

The bank angle indicator also contains the beacon indicator for the appropriate takeoff runway, so, to prevent its loss from the redesigned bank angle indicator, the runway beacon indicator could be relocated in the middle of the now redesigned bank angle indicators for left and right, allowing the pilots to not miss the appropriate runway.

Testing

Judging by how many new design and structural changes are being recommended here, it would important to carry out the appropriate and intensive testing, to get the right and fine-tuned mixture of all the desirous features. The procedural and training aspects are far less challenging to implement, only at the matter of cost and sacrificing some flying time and profits to get pilots the training that they need in rare but highly dangerous situations.

Conclusion

It is important that such measures (and any others necessary) take place by legislative fiat or by company action, whether by the company executive or worker decision and feedback.

Incorporating these and many more adjustments to the craft would allow for planes to, if not perfect at airborne survival, then be as darn close as possible to it, as possible is by human effort and ingenuity. That is my sincerest belief.

A Specific Synthesis Of Religion And Science

Opinion Piece

Oftentimes when we hear of a synthesis of Religion and Science, the most popular representations of such conversations are videos on Youtube where scientists and theologians/priests/spiritual healers/gurus/ etc. all come together to discuss generally accepted moral issues which even the average Liberal thinking fellow would agree with and that general feeling of connection with the cosmos, people and the world, even if the foundations of those agreements maybe different (convergence from parallels).

I'm not trying to diminish this connection, conversation and conclusion, this is because it matters to some or many people, however, if we are to talk about a more serious synthesis, moving beyond the conclusions of the Renaissance Men, the theologian/philosopher scientists of the past, the Illuminati (in its original 17th century memory of the intellectual society which saw Isaac Newton as a member as well), Spinoza's God, etc.

It's not that complicated, in my essay "Is God A Blackhole", the traits of the various Gods and Goddesses and other such spiritual beings can be taken together put into matrices and cross- referenced with each other to come to a conclusion which can be likely inconclusive in of itself if we try to study for them in the great beyond. However, to move beyond this limited synthesis of religion and science, we can think and explore a greater meaning and synthesis which involves trying to start with instrumentation which can measure the impact and presence of civilizations in the Universe who are so advanced, that their energy signals are at the level of the Universe and indistinguishable at our present technological level. To find those signals from the noise, we already have a map of the sky through the Cosmic Background Radiation map.

We can expand this search to examine, why a few UFOs are aliens and why they're visiting Earth and that they are of so many different technological capabilities, it's likely that the Earth is rare, such a lush, watery, minerally rich and dense planet must be rare in the Universe. In our search of exoplanets, 5,000 and counting, seldom is there a planet with the conditions of Earth, in fact, an exact Earth copy is non-existent, although better sensing equipment may change that in the future. The middle TRAPPIST planets (d, e, f), K2–18b, Gliese 186, and others are close Earth Analogues, but not exact [moderate temperatures (<100), organic molecules, liquid water, etc.) but they don't match our characteristics exactly, they might be too much or too little.

Anyways, the point of this, is that if we flex our brains to think about possibilities which may exist beyond the pale, then we can gradually come to examine entities that are divine. If we can examine interdimensional and extragalactic and ultra-advanced alien civilizations, we may have the pieces of the puzzle ready which can help us understand grander constructs in the Universe or beyond it, like God. Once we can figure out how things far more advanced then us exist or are, then very special frames or planes of existence that may exist may become clearer to us from a scientific perspective.

For example, sufficient energy in chemistry and biology could allow us to move between Universes, but the requirements would be so high, that it would be cost prohibitive, and much better to do it through physics. Similarly, using faith to understand science and vice-versa might be possible, but cost prohibitive, similarly studying such high-energy forces in the Universes may give us the tools to break the divide between faith and science, which work with different mechanisms, so that we can gain a truly fundamental understanding of the Universe.

This would represent a true synthesis between Science and Religion, the kind that you would not hear mostwheres.

And we are never too late to begin, due to our hesitation or the predominance of materialist thought in much of the world (how did our ancestors survive or even thrive in some instances, when the world was supposedly more materially and technologically poor? How did they raise so many children, if many and technology were at a much lower level? You may say with great difficulty or many children died, that maybe true, but outside of large-scale famines or disasters that affected the world, many people lived quite good lives, it might be because of a sense of communal well-being and harmony, of working and sharing together inspite of the odds, the difficulties and so on, a sense of the world that is largely disappearing from ours, as we become overreliant on technology and hoarding resources instead of sharing them, the moral and ethical values which allowed life to thrive in difficult circumstances have lapsed, and not by some natural and organic evolution, by the preponderance of those who realized that atomizing people, breaks their collective power and nothing has been more successful in this endeavour, than seeing people as rigidly in individual terms, rather than individuals part of a greater whole, individual rights granted by many states, while commendable, have also seen the dissolution of the collective spirit, while converting people into raging egotists, or if these passions always existed, then rewarding people to be so in the modern times and economic forces).

PS: While one of my cousins made an excellent thesis of a geographical, geological and anthropological nature, which works on these same lines of integrating science and spirituality, although it is more of a confirmation of global warming through parallel but complementary analyses, than a true synthesis, it is pretty good in interdisciplinary terms. However, it is a niché thesis outside of his very narrow circle, even though celebrated in it and referenced in the IPCC assessments. There needs to be a concerted and cheaper, more accessible and less niché approach to science-spirituality synthesis, beyond the mere integrative, while that implies a closer relation than strict secularism, a good example would be to bring two pieces of paper with different explanatory arguments close together from far apart and even stitch them together with a few connective words, synthesis would be them on the same page, exploring, understanding and enhancing explanatory power of reality together.

Examples:

1. In one essay of mine, I examined the question of, "Is God a blackhole?".

2. Even in a seemingly incompatible space, of Young Earth Creationism, we can, if we eschew literalism and rigidity of definitions on both sides of the religion-science "divide", we can take the lesson from Hinduism, that a day on God's World, a day of eternity, to put it more poetically, could be easily longer than a day on Earth, so 6,000 years or even 6 days could mean 13 or 14 billion.

3. Evolution as has been suggested earlier is not incompatible with intelligent design if we consider deistic evolution, whether soft (God merely initiated it, like the many animal forms of God in Hinduism) to hard (that God is the guider of evolution).

4. The figure of 8.4 million species in Hindu texts, falls in the range estimated by scientists.

With these examples, I intend to establish, that if both dogmatic scientists and religious folks loosen up their definitions and explanations, a true synthesis and grander understanding of reality is possible.

Bringing New Emotions To Nude Art

Add Muchness To Nude Art

Feel That Passion? Bring That Here.

Statue of Naked Woman among Trees, Loreta M, Gothenburg, Sweden Pexels.com

Emotions that which have been covered in nude art include fear, disgust, joy, appreciation, lust, paraphilic, eroticism, fine art-ism, etc. In its spirit various historical and ideological movements have also pursued nudity for aesthetics, idealism, strength, etc. Whether they are the Classical, Rennaisance, Romantic or Modern Nude art.

Ideologies which have contributed to Nude art can be Socialism, Liberalism, Traditional nudity in conservatism (The One-breasted personification of France, or the divine nudity of Gods in Hinduism), Fascism, Feminism and other such fields of inquiry.

However, what seems to be missing or largely absent are feelings like subtle-self-pleasure (not the pornographic), if at the very least to create an alternative in India about the "boob squeeze" scene which has been held up by censors in an Indian movie. This is perhaps to be expected in a country where nudity is present on some temples, while suggested nudity is blasted in cinema (outside of blue cinema) or rioted against. More flexibility even if controversial is present through the consumption of media on personal internet apps. Something like this can be present just to break the mold, for example here.

Other emotions which could exist are the more common but still rare, the playful as seen here and the unsettling (not horror, disgust, but one which implies threat but there may not be any) as seen here, there could be a threat to the baby, but it may not be anything. Threatening things that may within may not be threatening at all, the basis for the unsettling.

Other expressions or emotions include the surreal (first and second and trihd), the cheeky (first, second and third), the silhouette (1, 2, 3), cubist surreal, physical intimacy and succour and lastly but not least, a beautiful face staring directly at you or near you with eyes either partially or fully open, which suggests nudity or not, as seen in the following:

1. Violent Satisfaction
2. Sultry Nature
3. Trapped Within Your Own Machinations
4. Suggestive Bathing
5. Naiad
6. Quizzical Glare/Look
7. Music With Matte or Impressionist Background (Can also count as surreal, but mildly)
8. Dominance 1, Dominance 2
9. Contrast 1, Contrast 2

And so on, there is much more from where that came from, and we can discuss the finer nuances or links to more pics in our DMs if you so wish to communicate with me.

Nude art in India has remained a quiet and taboo, outside of the traditional religious art and motifs, where it is a selectively legal activity, taking inspiration from these kinds of photos may allow India to branch out and create unique art, simultaneously grounded in Indian culture and tradition while evolved and ahead of the world.

This would be a great way to move forward, even if at a surface level. Surface level progress is greater than no progress, if nude art has not changed in Universities for hundreds of years, and in the common imagination for thousands of years, with this foundation, a deeper evolution of nudity could be achieved.

(Visit the article on Medium to follow the links)

(Assume links to be nude art, all images linked herein are for personal consumption, you are appealed to not spread them if you download them or charge money for them, having said that, those actions are at your discretion, good luck :))

Can "Fascist Socialism" Exist?

TLDR: It is mostly theoretical. OPINION PIECE

(Author's Warning: The term "Fascist Socialism" here is not related to the usage by American "Conservatives" as a label for all or most forms of socialism, here it refers to the use of welfare or welfaristic, socialist or socialistic, communist or communistic policies and economic organization used by various Fascist nations in history, and can be extrapolated to modern Fascist or Neo-Fascist movements. It does not also take away from historical leftist ideologies, nations and movements which were authoritarian/totalitarian and do blur the lines. Fascism is the umbrella term which includes both pro and anti-nazi strands. I used the term conservative in quotations for Americans, because outside of some social policies related to conservatism, American conservatives, are conservatives for America, in a predominantly Liberal, large 'L', country, which has a history of what some might call a fixation with Liberty, but which Americans know in their hearts is the defining trait of their nation. American conservatives are not conservatives in the objective sense, they are actually, almost exclusively 90– 99% of the time radical, anti-statist, free-market capitalists who pay lip service to a very foolish and surface level interpretation

of social and cultural conservatism. They may be called "Libertarians", which is also a uniquely American and European and Western modern anomaly, as Libertarian actually meant a socialist anarchist in the early 20th century, before it was co-opted by the radical

free-marketeers in the 1950s US, if you really want to understand what true conservatism is, you have to go back to the pre-industrial past, to statesmen like Burke, Disraeli, movements like the Diggers, etc. if you're looking more recently in the west, Tolkein, Chesterton, Belloc, etc are good examples of old-fashioned Western Conservatism. Socialism involves the social ownership of the means of production and can involve the government but is not exclusive to it, it can be community or enterprise based among other forms of collective/social ownership).

Black Front Flag (Strasserism) FugeeCamp Public Domain Wikimedia Commons

There were a few Fascists who promoted economic socialism in their Fascism, mostly former socialists like Marcel Deat from France, Giorgio Pini from Italy, and the most prominent, the Strasser Brothers and Ernst Rohm in Germany. While French, British, Italian and Spanish Fascism tolerated economic socialism emanating from the working class which didn't challenge the authority of the state, the broader socialist movements at large were heavily repressed and crushed. Especially so in Nazi Germany, which outside of some leisure and welfare among the Nazi-determined appropriate German worker, they entirely abolished any pretence at redistribution and removed all those who could in the night of the long knives.

This blurring of lines and borrowing from different philosophical schools, is what makes it hard to pin down Fascism. But Fascism, except for some fringe elements within, rejects a radically socialist political economy, although, as mentioned earlier, it may tolerate some worker driven, politically unchallenging Socialist economics, independent of the mainstream Fascist party.

If co-ops were there in Nazi Germany, I know not of them.

While it is also true that central planning, a war economy, a saving-focus for salarymen which also dampened inflation, rationing, price controls, worker allocation by state, some welfare and gifts of consumer goods to placate workers, a single state managed worker union, etc. coexisted with private business, private property and a fiat currency and unconventional fiscal and monetary policy like the

MEFO Bills, complicates the picture of whether or not the Nazis were socialists, while one could certainly and cogently argue that while some of these policies were state socialistic and a few state communistic, it was the realities of war or ideological control that the Nazis desired (and for the most part, got) and the german cultural propensity to save and aversion to inflation which guided them, it could also be that Hitler now having placated the capitalists, having purged the socialists in his party, he had to offer the people and the workers something, when he had promised them total revolution and radical change.

It should also be remembered that many prominent Fascists were previously socialist, Benito Mussolini, Oswald Mosley, or used socialists as a defence against competing Fascists, such as when Kurt Schussnigg released socialist and communist prisoners to bolster support against the Austrian Nazi Party and pressure from Hitler, although it was too little, too late.

However, what this shows is that the relation between socialists and fascists is not as cut and dry as we would have been made to believe.

Some call Stalinism and Maoism a kind of Socialist Fascism, in unideological critiques, because they shared many traits with plain old fascism, ethnonationalism, Stalin's antisemitism, concentration camps, totalitarianism, genocide, mass purges, induced famines for cultural revolution and rapid industrialization, cult of personality, mass mobilization, ultranationalism, militaristic expansionism, etc. until they were replaced by more conservative, relatively moderate and inward focused administrations, those of Khrushchev and Deng Xiaoping.

And it needn't be reminded that Stalin and Mao (pol pot and others included), eliminated all those who opposed them, socialist or not, much like Hitler. Yet, one could quite honestly say that Stalin was the most thorough, killing off the largest number of groups of peoples, regardless of their classification, even if his absolute numbers weren't the most.

North Korea has removed Communism from its constitution, and has kept almost all Stalinist measures and traits (with a few differences and pauses, a little bit of market activity, a little bit of increase in consumer goods and light industry, a large increase in housing expenditure, a low to moderate increase in agricultural spending, a few mass produced goods, a pause to militaristic expansion through the armistice; although this might be changing, etc. but these are very minor changes, just tinkering on the edges of the system, nothing concrete).

North Korea even so, has kept its command economy, as dysfunctional as it is, because it maintains control over the people and has no interest in a socialist command economy that works for the common citizen. When it suits them, they adopt socialist rhetoric to suppress markets and regain control, when it suits them, they allow markets, to gain "indirect taxes". Much like their mobilization of the people for projects deemed nationally important are a form of "indirect taxation". So, the abolition of taxes is only nominal. The atheist state has a hereditary homo-divine figure as its head (here homo means human, not homosexual), who also presides for his ancestor's wishes, his father and his grandfather, creating a cult of personality and mythology around him of the kind, that can safely describe him as a God- Emperor of the old mould.

His economy system is a cross between a narco crime syndicate with feudal elements (in conjunction with a command economy), yet has very little to provide the people, unlike true feudal states, where there was much more decentralization and give and take. Most Crimes are punishable by death, to keep control, but the Supreme Leader still makes emotional appeals to his people to garner their support and allegiance, even if there may not be any significant change. The level of destitution in NK, leads to hostile land or property grabs, or people selling themselves or their homes for food, mimicing the most rapacious forms of capitalism in a nominally socialist state, the cultural and social homogeneity of the nation, strictly enforced etc. etc. etc. I could go on forever...but if opportunism is taken as the sole definition of Fascism, then NK is the best example of a Fascist state, probably ever. As most other fascist states were defined by their own kind of idealism, but NK represents using any method, from hereditary confinement in concentration camps for collective and consecutive lifetimes, to supporting markets, free-trade, foreign investment, etc. if it suits them.

Truly the best Fascist state if there ever was one.

In concluding, to avoid this confusion in the future, it is better to think of Fascism as a political or governance system like a Monarchy, and for socialism to be thought as the economic system.

As Discussed Above,

Can a Monarchist be a socialist? Yes. Can a socialist be a Monarchist? Yes. Is Monarchism, Socialism, and Vice-Versa, No.

Similarly,

Can Fascists be socialists? Yes. Can Socialists be Fascists, yes. Is socialism, fascism? No. Is fascism socialism? No.

It is important to demarcate political organization from economic organization, even if they're related as a political economy.

An example: maybe fascist socialism is more rigid and inflexible than more "liberal" or "open-minded" forms of socialism.

At a psychological level they are also not incompatible because different sub-ideological strands in Socialism and Fascism harbour what can be called, "anti-introception". Or the rejection of the emotional (feelings, introception, not introspection, a subtle but important difference). Marxist socialism, even though it has some minor romantic elements ("warmth of feudal socialism, denounced immediately afterwards or the alienation from one's own work under capitalism, critiquing the commercialization of the family too), etc., is stridently materialist in its analysis and non-esoteric forms of Fascism reject "too much feeling" too.

Capitalism And Free Money Are Compatible

Contrary to popular belief, capitalism and free money are compatible

Opinion Piece

Ayn Rand on Government Welfare and why those who oppose it are the ones who are most entitled to it (Snopes.com):

"In 2010, freelance writer Patia Stephens reported obtaining a Social Security Administration record via FOIA request showing that Ayn Rand collected a total of

$11,002 in Social Security payments between 1974 and her death in 1982 (her husband, Frank O'Connor, also collected benefits until his death)." "Yet the accusation of hypocrisy rests on an assumption that nowhere in Rand's vast oeuvre had she ever made a case for accepting money from the government. However, she did, in fact, make such a case in a 1966 essay, "The Question of Scholarships." It is morally defensible for those who decry publicly-funded scholarships, Social Security benefits, and unemployment insurance to turn around and accept them, Rand argued, because the government had taken money from them by force (via taxes). There's only one catch: the recipient must regard the receipt of said benefits as restitution, not a social entitlement. "Those who advocate public scholarships [or Social Security benefits] have no right to them; those who oppose them have," Rand wrote. In fact, she seemed to see it as something approaching the duty of those opposed to the redistribution of wealth to accept such payments: Since there is no such thing as the right of some men to vote away the rights of others, and no such thing as the right of the government to seize the property of some men for the unearned benefit of others — the advocates and supporters of the welfare state are morally guilty of robbing their opponents, and the fact that the robbery is legalized makes it morally worse, not better. The victims do not have to add self- inflicted martyrdom to the injury done to them by others; they do not have to let the looters profit doubly, by letting them distribute the money exclusively to the parasites who clamored for it. Whenever the welfare-state laws offer them some small restitution, the victims should take it." "Precisely because Rand views welfare programs like Social Security as legalized plunder, she thinks the only condition under which it is moral to collect Social Security is if one "regards it as restitution and opposes all forms of welfare statism" (emphasis hers). The seeming contradiction that only the opponent of Social Security has the moral right to collect it dissolves, she argues, once you recognize the crucial difference between the voluntary and the coerced. Social Security is not voluntary. Your participation is forced through payroll taxes, with no choice to opt out even if you think the program harmful to your interests. If you consider such forced "participation" unjust, as Rand does, the harm inflicted on you would only be compounded if your announcement of the program's injustice precludes you from collecting Social Security. This being said, your moral integrity does require that you view the funds only as (partial) restitution for all that has been taken from you by such welfare schemes and that you continue, sincerely, to oppose the welfare state." "The flaw in this argument is that it only adds up if you accept Rand's characterization of involuntary taxation as "legalized plunder" and her assertion that it confers upon those who object to it on principle (and, by some interpretations, only those who object to it on principle) the right to financial restitution. Flawed or not, however, the fact that she articulated the position puts paid to the charge that her acceptance of Social Security benefits in later life was hypocritical. On her own terms, it was not."

Source:

https://www.snopes.com/fact-check/ayn-rand-social-security Milton Friedman and Helicopter Money:

"Friedman himself refers to financing transfer payments with base money as evidence that monetary policy still has power when conventional policies have failed, in his discussion of the Pigou effect, in his 1968 AER Presidential address. Specifically, Friedman argues that "[the] revival of belief in the potency of monetary policy was strongly fostered among economists by the theoretical developments initiated by Haberler but named for Pigou that pointed out a channel — namely changes in wealth— whereby changes in the real quantity of money can affect aggregate demand even if they do not alter interest rates". Friedman is clear that money must be produced "in other ways" than open-market operations, which — like QE — involve "simply substituting money for other assets without changing total wealth". Friedman references a paper by Gottfried Haberler written in 1952, where Haberler says: "Suppose the quantity of money is increased by tax reductions or government transfer payments, and the resulting deficit is financed by borrowing from the central bank or simply printing money."

Source:

https://en.wikipedia.org/wiki/Helicopter_money

If the most ardent supporters of Capitalism can conceive of and/or accept atleast in some way or form a kind of "free money", then how can "free money" destroy Capitalism as the Australian Think Tank, Centre for Independent Studies claims?

Davos Is The Illuminati

The Devil Is In The Details

Opinion Piece

People often construct conspiracy theories around the Illuminati, that it is this powerful cabal that controls the World and all the governments in it. However, the intellectual Illuminati which existed in the 17th Century and saw Isaac Newton as one of its members has since long ceased to exist.

If you do wish to partake in grand conspiratorial schemes in the World, I suggest that you turn your eyes to the Davos International Economic Forum, mistakenly called the World Economic Forum.

There you will find heads of state kowtowing to big business and the representatives of Global Multinational Multi-Trillionaire Companies and centi-billionaires.

You can clearly see this in action, when the President of Argentina is gushing in front of the World Economic Forum and chastizing socialism. And the massive cuts to spending in Argentina, is making the IMF seemingly orgasm with joy, along with all the captains of industry worldwide.

However, he may soon find that his friends, the IMF and the business barons are not his or his country's friends, their adherence to purist capitalist dogma is as weak as anyone else's who's a good businessman, judging by their dealings with China, Russia, Pakistan and his own country, he could cut his spending the basement and implode his country, the IMF and the barons wouldn't really magically boost their spending on investments. Indeed, for them to give money there has to be a state, which Argentina will likely remain, even if Milei wishes that he could dissolve it. The Barons like proper state investment, while they get to what they want, much like spoilt children, don't expect them to lavish Argentina with funds, just because spending will be in the ground, EU, US, China, are all behemoths of output and production, and they'd much rather put their money there. The IMF too, likes some austerity cuts for show, and then showers the target countries with money. The idealism Libertarianism, much like other idealisms has little place in the World of percieved pragmatism of these big players of the World.

Clearly, your energies would be better spent there, however, if somehow there is some cabal which is like the conspiratorial Illuminati, then I am not aware of it, and it is likely to be unlikely.

German Querfrot Inspired Radical Fascist Flag

Onion Piece

German Querfront Inspired Radical Fascist Flag

Borrowing from all Proto-Fascist Movements And Parties, created a fictional Radical Fascist Flag with my own ideas and unique elements.

Welcome your thoughts and feedback. :) Google drive link here:

https://drive.google.com/drive/folders/1VgxWvUgtUqksHIpzJPozapCdrfXR9b_I Thanks for your patience! :)

Content from outside and software used:

1. Canva Artistic Flag Template (rough):

    Search "flag" under template, scroll down to "Art On The Air" flag

2. Royal Lion Rearing Motif:
    https://images.app.goo.gl/1rPufRFLhmoH31GKA

3. Sparkling Sun:

    https://pixabay.com/photos/sun-sparkle-icon-shine-ray-star-2545670/

4. Used Image for Querfront as it showed up on Google, may have no real correlation, represents National Bolshevism instead, I think. Deviantart picture, cercle proudhon flag by NeoBolshevik:

    https://www.deviantart.com/neobolshevik/art/Cercle-Proudhon-flag-1045749495

5. Used OpenArt.ai for converting the symbol of Fasci d'Azione Rivoluzionaria:
    https://en.wikipedia.org/wiki/Fasci_d%27Azione_Rivoluzionaria#/media/File%3AEmblem_of_the_Fasci_d'Azione_Rivoluzionaria_(Milan).jpg

6. Dallas Cowboys Star Vector:

    https://www.vecteezy.com/free-vector/dallas-cowboys-star

7. Remaining graphics are from within the Canva app

8. The arrows of the falange:

    FET de la JONS:
    https://en.wikipedia.org/wiki/Falange_Espa%C3%B

lola_de_las_JONS#/media/File%3ABandera_FE_J ONS.svg

9. Wreath of wheat

   https://pixabay.com/vectors/corn-wheat-wreath-2024287/

How Aliens Get Here To Earth

Search And Be Found

Time Lapse Photo of Tunnel, by Burak The Weekender, Pexels.com

It is generally thought by many in the mainstream, that aliens cannot get here, after all how can such vast distances combined with the speed of light limit, be covered in a reasonably good time? Well, hold on to your butts, and let me gently, blow your mind away. :D

Many different kinds of technology and methods will be mentioned below, because the understanding is that not every civilization will be at the same level of advancement. This article assumes that a few UFOs observed, when compensating for all non-ETI possibilities are non-zero sourced from ET. Anywhere from 0 to 35% of all sightings, dependent on the study.

Enhanced Understanding Of The Casimir Effect

There are many stars in our vicinity which have planets in the habitable zone and are a billion or more years older than our star. What this means that it gives them the time to investigate matters and solve them, where our understanding is in its infancy. One of these issues in Physics is the Casimir Effect.

When two specially made metal plates are gradually put together in a vacuum, but never touching, it leads to a force which acts on them, implying negative energy.

In a vacuum quantum fluctuations keep happening, particle-anti-particle pair appear and disappear through annihilation shortly after coming into existence, which is why they are called "virtual particles". While the literature which exists on this topic can confuse the average reader, essentially, some of these particles in the pairs manage to escape the destruction process, but these are very few, leading to a diffuse "pressure" which is applied on the plates, bringing them together, likely because the closeness of the plates prevents the optimal movement of these particles, preventing a few of them from going through the annihilation process, or delaying it enough for said few particles to escape, much like the proposed Hawking Radiation emanating from Black Holes, except without the gravitational effects. These particles can be "normal" antimatter or matter, but some of these few have exotic properties like negative mass or negative energy.

The pressures exerted are equivalent to a force tens of thousands smaller than 1 Joule or even lower, making it a highly diffuse, unstable and difficult source of energy to harness. However, there is no restriction, that if countless years of research happen, there is nothing to prevent an advanced alien civilization from garnering the knowledge which is needed to magnify, enhance and trap the energy to exploit it as a sufficient energy source.

Starships which have rings of exotic matter wrapped around them, which are very thick (fat) and vibrating to reduce the energy requirements for the Alcubierre Warp Drive (there are other kinds) to manageable amounts, like 700–800 kgs approximately (1750–2000) pounds roughly), instead of the Universe's mass or that of Jupiter, as earlier calculations showed. Once this problem has been solved, the Aliens would scan the night sky and try to locate planets like ours, rare and precious blue marbles (assuming they aren't made of Silicon and Boron and instead Carbon, surely). Then sub-light starships attached with a negative energy/mass generator or generators attached to it, would lay "hyper- highways", which would end more than a light year outside of the solar system's furthest celestial bodies, like our Kuiper Belt. As it is theorized that the blast from the deceleration of an FTL capable starship would be atleast a light year in diameter (which would require testing of the drive in a very empty part of space, atleast 100 to 1000 light years of emptiness for an unmanned FTL starship). Then the FTL starship would move into the target Solar System, to move towards the target planet at sub- light speeds. Any effects on the Heliosphere by the deceleration blast, may need to be studied to prevent any potential harm to the habitability of the concerned system.

They would also have shielding if the FTL starship was manned, to prevent the damage to the crew and the ship interior from Gamma and X radiation, this could explain why radiation accompanies some UFO sightings, especially those which are reported to land, as the highly irradiated exterior of the ships would gradually reduce in radioactivity as they travel inside the solar system at sub-light speeds.

This could imply that very near planets could be visited by sub-light speeds, and the further away ones by FTL ships, if FTL ships are visiting our planet, this might imply some level of risk-taking, desperation or lack of concern and dangerous fly-boy or space-boy cowboy behaviour. Keeping to sub- light speeds and a reasonable distance from our outer solar system, could still imply careful navigating by our alien visitors.

Unmanned ships would also be easier to mass produce, as they have no need for heavy shielding, crew quarters, hibernation pods, etc. which could be one of the reasons behind their reported extreme accelerations and movements during sightings.

As for why they could be coming here, it's quite possible that they're nearby within 40–50 light years or less and that Earth is truly rare, how many of the over 5,000 exoplanets that we have observed would be like Earth? Very few, in the single digits if not less. Super-Earths and

Hycean Worlds may increase the number, but their gravities might be too uncomfortable for those beings used to the gravities of average rocky planets, anywhere from Mars or Ganymede and Mercury sized objects, to objects uptil

1.1 times Earth Mass (1–1.1).

Shapes such as the spherical, oval, roundish, tic-tac and so on, could be explained by the shielding required by the intense radiation levels present, which would be less necessary at sub-light speeds. Even machines need shielding from radiation which could be high (even if the needed shielding is relatively less).

The extreme energy levels and preparation times for such travel, would be an important consideration, which would require selecting the most appropriate planets, even if they have resident life like us.

Some older supernovae could be signs of warp drives which powered up in a place near us, in our interstellar vicinity.

Of course this doesn't explain why we can't see them come into our main or inner solar system, but this data could easily be classified by NORAD, NASA, etc. as to why private telescopes don't report it, it could be the ridicule factor, public-private collusion, burial under bureaucratic verbosity or some hithereto unknown reason (cloaking, stealth?) besides them not coming here of course.

Wormhole Drives And Gateways

The other reason behind why UFO sightings report such extreme and hypercapable maneuverability and speeds unaccompanied by sonic booms without the craft having a smooth and long cone for a nose, is quite likely because they may use Wormhole Drives. The Negative matter and energy which allows for the use of Warp Drives, also allows stabilizing Wormholes, or could be found inside stable wormholes, either natural or artificial. More exotic properties of the Universe, such as antigravity could also be used, which could imply an understanding of the Universe's fundamentals beyond that of a Unified Theory of Gravity (as imagined by us).

Such Wormhole, gravity/antigravity drives could allow for more regular or irregular shapes that which we have noticed, which differ from the ones seen by those which could be powered by Warp Drives.

There could also be gateways, or portals, which are artificial wormholes, could be present somewhere in our solar system.

Dimensional Drives

If there are visitors from other dimensions, higher or lower, but likely higher, since there might be a limit to how few physical dimensions proteins could function in effectively for life and biology to exist. Lower dimension Universes may dead in terms of life how we recognize it, but Flatland should prevent dissuasion in y'all.

These dimensional drives could imply parallel existence in our same Universe and/or multiversal beings which travel between Universes and Dimensions.

As an example, these drives could explain something at the edge of our ability of comprehension. These drives could allow travel through physical 4D blackholes or greater, and to land up on their 3D or higher surfaces, that is where we are. If that is the case. Or travel from this higher-dimensional Universe to ours, without their ships being destroyed, through some mechanism unknown to us. Or there could be other ways of their travel through dimensions and/or universes.

This is speculative, but it could explain, why some UFOs seem to blink in and out of existence for RADAR and/or VISUAL observers. And why some of them have strange and constantly changing shapes, which could represent a 3-D cross-section of their real shape, as they interact with our Universe and/or Dimension.

Nuclear Rockets And Other Conventional Methods

Nuclear rockets, whether fission or fusion, and whether or not they're doped with antimatter, could tell us about the attitude of the alien civilization concerned and their level of advancement. It could mean that they put significant resources into their space programs, even if their world had conflicts like ours (or not), which would take away the limits of their comparatively low-tech, they would be very near to us in technological terms. We would understand that if not advanced, they believed in investing heavily into nuclear and space, their global warming levels maybe lower than ours, due to their possible higher usage of nuclear in energy production and transport. And it would be very, very interesting to find such interstellar generation starships as they would be enormous, unmistakable and relatively slow enough for us to view and track them quickly.

We could also find solar sail probes (allegedly like Oumuamua and others), chemical generation starships through Ion Drives and Magnetoplasmadynamic Thrusters (MPDTs), as these represent continuous thrust over long periods of time.

Basically Magic

Maybe their worlds had traits and properties, and their adaptations or exploitations of these could seem like magic to us or *are magic*.

Artifacts And Crafts

We have not in detail examined the entire solar system with a fine tooth comb, so much of it is still unknown to us, where a stealth, or even conventional artifacts and crafts could be hiding or squirreled away.

Von Neumann Machines

These machines, self-replicating in nature could be as proposed, helping to quietly or loudly spread alien presence and influence in our neighbourhood or the galaxy at large, such sentinels could be hiding or are hidden in our solar system, away from our prying eyes, till we search for them.

Deep Time

There are very few if any ways for us to find artifacts in the long past of geological time, whether aliens visited our world, unless they have been preserved in very sturdy materials like Quartz, as deep time could've destroyed them, or they deliberately left subtle chemical isotopic and allotropic signatures in pieces of Quartz with curious kinds of chemical make-up and mixtures waiting to be found.

Search And Be Found

If we look for such technosignatures close to home, we should find them.

How Liberalism Ate Itself

Liberalism stagnates and eats itself when dominant, uninteresting Experiencing the challenge to Liberalism Within A Western University

Opinion And Anecdotal Piece

For Libel Reasons I will not give the name of the artist or the University, I shall be oblique. For the University, I'll mention the time range, if you happen to see my Linkedin Page and connect the dots, that's not my fault.

As for the artist, I will mention her actions, if you can figure out who it is, that's not my fault.

I was at a British University by remote in 2020–21, studying Filmmaking there.

In one such of the meetings of meeting artists from outside, I came across a session where a French artist mentioned how she in the '70s stalked people and then asked them to come into her home to photograph them while they slept.

Leaving aside the fact that this is illegal and a tad bit creepy, it was possible that the artist could've been harmed or, the people didn't know the artist's intentions, they could've been harmed.

An MA Photography student was then asked to carry out a similar assignment.

In my initial complaint, I asked the University to not host such meetings in the future and to prevent such assignments. Obviously not the best tactic, in my later, cooler view. I re-phrased the complaint to make it more about safety and progressivism, trying to test the supposed Liberal ideal of Universities, especially in the West.

Of course, this is a different University and a different country, the UK, maybe they're less oriented towards safetyism than the US. However for the COVID pandemic we were supposed to write a good number of safety documents, perhaps it lead to the false belief that the University was dedicated to safety.

The University's complaint process was bureaucratic and the watchdog only had power to bring back lost money, not carry out any real change.

Perhaps the only reason they followed the Legal rules around the COVID pandemic, was because of the way the state strongly enforced it.

To their credit, the head of media gave me the space to speak, even if one of my professors was visibly aggravated by my stance and complaint, he told me, the HOD continuously that this had been vetted by various committees, ethics, don't know the exact names of the others (but likely of various concerned departments), etc. however is something okay just because the bureaucratic procedures have been satisfied?

Are there no moral questions or moral concerns? Are there no internal conversations with your conscience to guide your actions, are you an uninquisitive, insentient machine that just does what it is told or follows an internal schematic for action?

Perhaps you need to reconsider your actions, when a generative chatbot AI has a better conscience than you.

I withdrew my complaint and withdrew from the University, while it was a futile gesture, atleast they would no longer get money.

Indeed, it seems as if in the pursuit of greater freedoms, lesser restrictions on the individual and always following the new fad, Liberalism has eaten itself and has morphed into the kind of unphilosophical "Libertarianism", of "If I ask you, then it's okay", like the consent driven murder in the "Syndic".

Back in the day, Liberal meant something, challenging paradigms, pushing the boundary, questioning everything, not accepting things as given, etc. A ruthless critique of everything, including itself.

Perhaps it is a victim of its own success, that the only thing it has left, is illegality and "amorality".

Marquis De Sade had sex slaves, Casanova slept with his daughter, the French Artist stalked people in the '70s, atleast be original in your illegality, open the coffers of the University and distribute the money to the starving masses, steal from yourself, atleast then you will be original in your immorality. Somewhat.

And I think that if the Guardian cannot be bothered to investigate this, even if we assume that they have the paucity of time to investigate all scandals, one cannot be surprised that they would not pursue this, because Universities are their constituent groups, they are beholden to them.

Let's create uninteresting, bureaucratic, amoral and socially and psychologically and emotionally inept filmmakers, yes, that would solve everything! Atleast the Nazis could offend you and have grandiose plans and visions, the only grandiose plans these inept bureaucrats would have is their own suicide and the mass murder of others, let them toss themselves into the garbage bin of History, that is the best remedy.

How To Be A Popular Rightist In A Liberal Democracy

Also Known As The Ideology Most of The Billionaire Class Is Scared Of

In this short book, I will provide the ideological makeup and suggestions about how an individual or a group of individuals can create a broad-based right-wing movement, by combining disparate ideological currents into itself to likely create a new, unique and historically unparalleled Right-Wing movement which should be able to answer the critiques levied at Right-Wing Thought by Left, Liberal and Libertarian intellectuals and outmaneuver them electorally, politically and morally as well. And to provide a serious challenge for other boring and pedantic mainstream pseudo-populist Right-Wingers in other countries as well.

Be advised that while these ideas have come from me, from my research, they have been fine-tuned by assistance from the AI software, Chatgpt 3.5. Which for its supposed liberal and left slant, is useful as a large database for knowledge, to fine tune philosophical arguments.

As with any political movement, this will require decades of hardwork and grassroots activism to result in a meaningful outcome on the local and national stage. Some of the views here maybe unpopular within your respective country, but the whole point of a movement is to foster a national realignment of ideology in due time.

Read on if you wish to understand a kind of conservatism which extends beyond merely saying no and the status quo.

How Will The Ideological Structure Of This Movement Be?

1. Agrarianism

The movement will aim to have a strong base in the rural part of the country, whether or not there are lot of people who are employed in the agricultural sector or not, nor whether the GDP is made up by agriculture or not. For the simple and practical reason that if your farmers are not happy, they can easily stop making food for the country, and then where will you be?

While ideally, land in the rural part of the country should be used on a co-ownership basis, it may be that your rural populations are against such redistribution, so what should be the steps taken?

Simple, in general, advocate for local decision making and greater autonomy for farmers and other productive rural forces.

In specific, try to make people form connections that exist beyond mere economic competition, to emphasize the bond between rural folk. People will then naturally gravitate towards more sharing of land and resources as they increase their trust in each other (as you would expect in a large family).

This also means that those who live closest to Nature, whether tribal or otherwise should get first priority on how to best preserve and exploit Nature.

2. Paternalistic Conservatism

Also known as Conservative Socialism, Feudal Socialism or Old-Fashioned Conservatism. A common mistake that most conservatives the World over make (with a few exceptions like Evo Morales and a handful of other populist conservatives in the World), is that a radically free-market will somehow promote the environment for a planet where people will overcome their aggressive individualism and magically embrace social conservatism and community values (communitarianism), this if I needn't spell it out to you dear reader, is an impossibility, a populace primed for decades to only be concerned for its own material and hedonistic pleasures, will not, if given the chance, start to care about their fellow man, if given even more economic freedoms, it's more like that in their most beneficial form, they may be a harmless incarnation of Elon Musk, but in their most nefarious form, a bitter ideologue like Mr. Trump.

The only kind of conservatism that can "resolve" this fake contradiction in modern "conservatism", is that of the old kind.

Back in the past, conservatives understood that for a beneficient society, where life in all its stages can be respected and protected whether unborn or born, it has to be in the arms of a caring government, a modest society, a loving family and a good community, where children, the elderly, pregnant women and any other, as economics would say, "non-productive" member of society could find succour.

Liberate yourselves from the faux populism of neoliberals who have taken up the currently hollow mantle of "cultural nationalism" which merely manifests as xenophobia, bigotry and hatred to win your disgruntled and angry votes, while they simultaneously proclaim self-righteously that they are "anti- woke", "anti-big business", etc. When they are infact none of these things.

Do not fall into the trap of the culture wars, whereas in the 19th century they were minor and short- lived, as Bismarck divorced himself from the concept of the Church's influence on state policy, a foregone conclusion post-french revolution, the present culture wars are unending and perpetually fractuous, pitting the supposed "woke" and the "anti-woke" against each other.

Leave the immigrants, sexual, religious and gender minorities alone, fighting with them just because their lifestyles repel you, merely allows you to become a tool in the culture wars, to exhaust your political power in futiling arguments about who's right and who's wrong, exactly what the powers that be want, a divide and rule policy, so that they can continue to get rich off of your collective dissatisfaction and frustration at the system, while they go scot-free. Focus your energies instead on creating durable grassroots religious and patriotic groups which want to bring about real change, which includes advancing family values, rural livelihoods, reindustrialization and other such good, whole of society endeavours, which bring back vitality and growth into society, while not demonizing minorities, or as they're better known, your fellow humans. Like fraud and thievery, the divide and conquer method has worked throughout history, in pre and post democratic times. Consider yourselves rightly more informed and educated than to keep falling for these endless ouroboros-like battles which seem neverending and ceaseless and only work to absorb your anger at the system and redirect it at those who are mostly innocent of its negative outcomes, and are also its victims.

If you wish to win the culture wars, do not engage in them, ignore them, build your grassroots movement on the traditional values you wish to see and time will solve this contradiction. Foster a genuine society based on sincerity, fairness, compassion, respect, morality and other values that conservatives appreciate, and the outcomes of culture war will be apparent in a few decades time, rather than decided today, but rending the fabric of society limb from limb, atleast in the sections where such discussions matter.

3. Nominal "Authoritarianism" with Decentralization

Having a Monarch, limited by a constitution, election, tradition, or a combination of these factors, or having a traditionalist who acts so, is beneficial to a conservative project.

While many nations are Republics with Presidents and Prime Ministers, having a longer term senior executive of the nation, with more term limits (say 3 or 4 or more, as according to your local needs and wanta vs 2), allows stability and defactionalization in society. A President or Prime Minister who acts like a philosopher king, can control the intense passions of the people with a veto or selected passage of legislature. It is measures like these that ensure that the chance for extremism in society is diminished.

Nations with an electoral college, should enact protections for the electoral college, to ensure that the electors can vote with their conscience and not what their parties or subdivision electorates decide. Say if a state or other subdivision votes for a candidate that aims to dissolve the constitution of your country, the electors from that state should have the necessary constitutional protections, part of the basic structure which ensure that they will not be punished if they act to protect the constitution from extreme candidates, and countries which don't have this system should adopt it.

Senior executives of a nation (such as the President, Prime Minister and Cabinet) should be independents by law, so that they cannot be swayed by the demands of parties, and with caution enact laws that they think are the best for the country, with the appropriate checks and balances of parliament. This would be like the American system, but less party oriented. How the American founders would've liked it to have been.

Any such system should also practice departisanship, delegation of authority to governors, chief ministers, and other local leaders down to the smallest level, this will aid in efforts to debureaucratize the nation as well. The centralization of powers merely bogs the nation's vitality down in thousands of pages of regulation. As an example, the US has over twenty thousand volumes of regulations as part of the US Code accumulated over 270 years. Not all of it is currently active, yes, but it slows down the investigative and oversight powers of the government, if it is so large that it cannot even know what is going on in its own nether regions, it should not exist.

This also involves not dissolving states if you are a part of the national movement, merely creating more.

4. Market Socialism And True Economic Conservatism

If you believe in a Conservatism which opposes economic centralization of power, or at the very least is skeptical of it. Then the kind of conservatism which opposes big business (especially in its most rapacious form) and bureaucratic socialism, represented by Stalinism, Dengism and even modern social democracy, is an admirable goal to have. To oppose unhindered state and private power regardless of what form it takes.

The most beneficial form of economics, is the one which reduces government and private control over the common resources that we all share. And instead letting the community and the individuals that make it up to decide what to do with it.

This can be done without expropriation, by the simple encouragement, by subsidy, law and tax to form more cooperatives, and to orient private companies more towards their workers, till such time they themselves realize, as the managers of the Brazilian export company, Semco did (and the Chinese manufacturing company haier), that by involving their workers in the entire process through democracy, whether it be as small as hiring or as large as production, in fact increases output, efficiency and the quality of goods. This is because the workers who work with the very things they have been for ages, know what goes on at every level and understand how to get things done.

Yes, there are workers who would take advantage of this Good Faith, but that's a human condition, and not just a worker condition. The Companies can also decide that no subunit of their company will be larger than the number that it takes to make a particular amount of product. Haier makes sure that its subunits, dependent on their department, are no larger than 50–150, respectively, all these "cells", or as it's known in conservatism, Organicism, the natural evolution of social structures through an organic interaction with each other, will work in conjunction to run the company as a whole.

Now, of course, in institutions that need a strict hand, like a nuclear reactor, or appropriate deference to a Captain's greater experience on a plane, are examples of flexibility of approach, and shouldn't seek to diminish the importance of authority when needed.

Such economic decentralization and common control and democratization, will allow ideas to flow freely in our economic system, as they do in our social and political system, or in those that don't have them, gradually force a change in. This will reduce bureaucracy and authoritarian capitalism and socialism, which diminishes the individual and then eventually the society and community around them.

Even in highly capitalistic systems like the US, the Tennessee Valley Authority and the Alaska Common Fund show Dirty (as in dirty energy) but collective action which provides a common income and energy distribution and control system which works well for the people under them.

This approach will lead to a reindustrialization of society and a maintenance or growth of that industrialization.

Yes, it will be mostly focused towards light industry and consumer goods, but

A. That's what the people want more than anything else.

B. That's what a diversity of tactics is for, the government can handle heavy industry and infrastructure by knowing where investment needs to be directed, but there's no reason, where feasible, that a similar approach can't happen.

5. Defensive Militarism, Armed Neutrality, Semi-Isolation, Semi-Autarky, Limited Collaboration

It's important to expand the defence industry (not at the expense of others), and localize production in your nation, to protect your independence. This also results in a policy of Armed Neutrality.

Economic Nationalism and True Economic Conservatism as discussed earlier can only be possible, if we localize not only defence production, but all production. By this I mean that we (India) should leave the World Trade Organization within a particular time frame. After we have invested enough money, say a trillion dollars over 30 years to localize production of all kinds, and making independent trade deals with as many countries as we can, outside of the WTO, then we can seek to leave it, at a minimum. Such intense and large investment, should also have a government independent council of inspector generals formed by the Supreme Court to adjudicate on how to spend the money effectively and wisely, so as to ensure that we are ready in 30 years time, and to avoid the waste and corruption which was uncovered by the American inspector general overseeing the Iraq and Afghanistan reconstruction.

Financial Autarky is also highly important, holding Western Currencies only allows your nation to come under sanctions, if you do something which the West dislikes. It would be wise for India to accrue Brazilian Real and South African Rand, as an alternative to Chinese, Russian or Western Currency. For countries that are allied to the West, China or Russia, these could be valid alternatives, otherwise, for neutral countries, it would be advisable to make these independent bilateral links.

As with the UN, it is a US and Great Power dominated institution, which has teeth, only when they will it so, it would be much better for any neutral and sovereignty loving country to gradually extricate itself from the UN, to be an observer nation and continue to selectively follow its international goals and fund programs that nations find good, it would be alright to maintain the UN institutions already present within your country, if they're doing good work.

It would be preferable along with this to create alternate bilateral and multilateral institutions.

Keep your military defensive, and be accepting of refugees, in light of the BJP's faux nationalism, the religion based immigration amendment, did nothing to alleviate the troubles of Hindus persecuted in Bhutan, Myanmar and Sri Lanka, as they are sensitive countries over whom influence is contested by China.

True Nationalism, mixed with conservatism, would be to accept refugees regardless of who they are (as long as they satisfy anti-terrorism scrutiny), as Germany did with accepting a million refugees. Yes, you could say that it was a cynical ploy to keep Germany's economy afloat, but if so, it was a very expensive cynical ploy, wouldn't you say? Compassion should re-enter the conversation about conservatism, you cannot be truly conservative or religious, without practicing compassion.

Don't neglect your citizen's needs as only those who can look after themselves can look after others. This includes a favourable birth rate, an economy which works for everyone, and institutions that are agile and effective, not mired in decades of bureaucratic rules.

Once your nation's local production and consumption is satisfied, you can drop all barriers to trade, even if you have exited the WTO, because people in your nation, would be so appreciative of the quality of your local goods and services, that they wouldn't even bother with cheaper but inferior goods from abroad.

I would suggest that Supranational Union likes the Eurasian Economic Union, USMCA (NAFTA successor), The South American Economic Union, ASEAN, TPP, the European Union, the African Union, etc., may not allow for such "radical" atleast from the neoliberal (or the new classical liberal) outlook, hence I advise that you leave such institutions and deals to foster growth and vitality at home. Do it in a time frame that would not harm your citizens or your sovereignty, so do it when you're ready and your local conditions allow you too.

6. Anti-Extremism And Inclusive Social Conservatism or Ethical Conservatism

If it didn't need to be spelt out before, avoid extremism. Guard against it. Especially ideologies or aspects of them that negate the value of life, whether through mass murder, like Nazism, Stalinism, Maoism, Religious Extremism, Abortion, like many advocates of Liberalism, Death from Poverty like in unrestricted capitalism, or like violent subsets of Anarchism, which seek change through violent revolution. Anarchism can be a great ally of Conservatism, due to its similar critiques of concentrated power. The state is a servant of the people, not its master. We can seek inspiration from many advocates of religious anarchism, like Gandhi, Tolstoy and Martin Luther King Jr.

However he who fights monsters must not become a monster himself. To avoid abortion, don't penalize women, find out why women are aborting foetuses, there maybe very few who are doing it entirely for internal reasons than for external reasons, if they are doing it for solely internal reasons, try to use moral persuasion rather than force. Good cannot be forced on people, only when people have the freedom to choose from Good or Evil can Good truly come about, otherwise it would be merely the pantomime of Good.

To avoid mass murder, seek a non-violent militancy that upholds the value of life, and defends the defenseless against tyranny, do not use strength to victimize people, use it to protect people, that is the true symbol of strength.

Those who carry out mass murder, may think that they are powerful, but they are merely cowards who hide behind the state and weapons of mass destruction (including guns), the only true weapon, is your body, to protect those who can't protect themselves. Think of Aikido, you turn the force of your enemy against himself, you do not hurt your enemy, you show your enemy that his violence can only harm himself and not others.

As Barry Goldwater said, Extremism in pursuit of virtue is no vice and moderation in pursuit of vice is no virtue.

Be as Martin Luther King Jr. said, be an extremist for love. I am an extremist, but an extremist for love.

For those who think that this is idealism, I would like to remind you of the national movement that Mahatama Gandhi created for freedom inspired by Tolstoyan thought, and MLK Jr. who was inspired by Gandhi to strive to break Jim Crow with non-violence and civil disobedience.

The Kingdom of God has always been within you, you just have to be open to it.

The means and ends are not separate from each other. Means also matter more than ends, but they are both important.

7. Soft-Secularism and Non-Violent Militancy

Adherence to religion is not anti-democracy, we can have within our government respect and accommodation for religion without forcing it on others. Encourage religious institutions that help people and further encourage the evolution of religious thought, in temples, churches, dargahs, mosques, gurudwaras, synagogues, fire temples, etc.

Have a non-violent militia which protects people and the way of life that fosters the flourishing of it.

8. End

When I said that this will be a popular rightism, it will be, but only in the long run and after lots of hard work and setbacks, but if achieved, it will repay handsomely, adapt to your local situations, encourage factionalism and internal democracy in this movement, it is only like this can long-lasting and beneficial change come about. A true Right-Wing Populism unlike the faux we see in the World today. This is the ideology that most of the billionaire class is afraid of, because they are either socially progressive and economically capitalist or socially conservative and economically capitalist and such, very few would advocate for such a morally upright bottom-up form of socialism or populism, if you prefer.

I ask you to join this movement of Total Revolution or Sampoorna Kranti, as Jayaprakash Narayana did in the mid-70's.

Thank You.

PS: Cultural Soft-Segregation And Protective Gender Segregation.

People generally self-segregate, so there's no urgent need to emphasize it. There should be protective segregation of women to protect them from assault as a conservative movement, but nothing needed on the scale of Saudi Arabia.

Within this system it would be important to add the semi-direct democratic system of citizen's referendum, seen in the Swiss and California Model and others. 😊

For more information on the ideological heritage of this ideology, you can look at Gandhi, Tolstoy, Dattopant Thengadi, Jayaprakash Narayana, Dadabhai Naoroji, C. Rajagopalachari, Burke, MLK Jr., Scruton, Marx, John Stuart Mill, Adam Smith and others.

How To Make Central Planning Work

A credible floor and ceiling for the economy

Opinion Piece

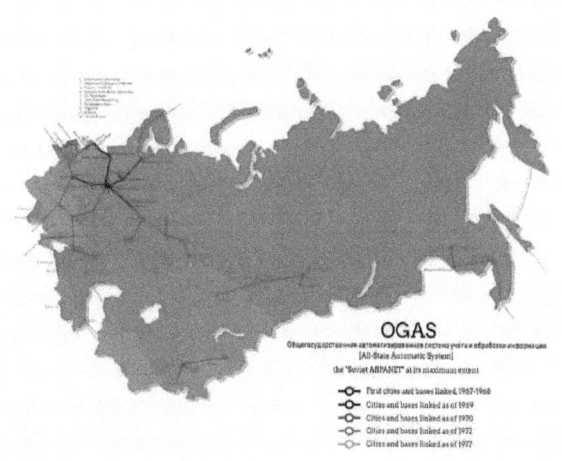

OGAS USSR (CCCP) Source: National automated system of computation and information processing: OGAS 2.0 — cibcom

Premise: If we assume that humanity will be around in 2 million years and more, and I see no reason why, if the dinos could be around for 150 million, there's no reason why we couldn't be, then in that period of time, inflation even if kept at a steady 2%, or we assume a more dynamic system, with ups, downs (from disasters or even civilizational collapse) and plateaus (marked by central banks or other controlling mechanisms), then it is easy to assume that inflation, barring some dramatic boosts in production or efficiency like a Galactic or extra-galactic civilization with a representatively large market, would see an inflation of unimaginable proportions necessitating a command economy at some point in human history, or some sort of central planning whether by the community in a more decentralized manner, or by the state, dependent on the ideology of the polity/polities which would exist in that period of time, or any time period in general from now till then and beyond. Of course, even if we have the resources of the entire Universe and God-like technology, there would still not be enough productive capacity in the Universe to handle the continuous expansion from millions of years of growth-led inflation. This is of course assuming that there is the possibility of FTL travel and communication. This is theoretically possible and given enough time, it could be that we have a governance system that can exert control over vast reaches of space through a practical application of such theoretical knowledge.

But if we assume that this is true and humanity continues to exist well into the future, then how would such a Centrally-Planned Economy function?

In the Soviet Union, the centrally-planned economy first used the martial power gained from the Russian Civil War to enforce the rapid collectivization of resources under the banner of War Communism, then it moved on to the NEP, which allowed some capitalistic measures to revive the economy, rapid collectivization and using brute force and brute violence allowed Stalin to make the Soviet Union into an industrialized state in 20–25 years. With Khruschev and Brezhnev came a selective Liberalization and Stabilization and finally with Gorbachev, came dissolution, because loosening control with losing the grip on the economy allowed centrifugal forces to spin the Soviet Union apart.

However, underneath this overarching story, there is the story of successful and advanced military goods which did not make their way into the civilian economy, due to secrecy, which inspite of its many inefficiencies kept the Soviet Union the second largest industrial power for much of the 20th century.

Among the experiments done along with the NEP (one could regard Stalin's collectivization an experiment too, conducted in another way it could've failed) and in the Tsarist experience of the command economy required for the first world war (which could've lead to the same kind of industrialization as Stalin, had it been uninterrupted, one could argue that the hardships suffered in 1917 were much lower and fewer than those faced in 1918–1923) and in the 1960's the proposal of the

OGAS, or the Soviet Internet as it is colloquially known, to modernize, accelerate, decentralize, debureaucratize and bring some efficiency and purposeful direction to the Soviet Economy, Kosygin's Reforms and other such attempts at acceleration before Gorbachev.

In Yugoslavia, there was a volatile, chaotic and a system for great potential for growth and great potential for failure, a system which combined markets, central planning, soviet and western aid, leading to a system influenced by all systems, yet not sticking to one. This lead to great growth, but also great volatility, for example, while enterprises were worker run, but were not worker owned, so wages rose, but not productivity and profitability at the scale needed, and so inflation crept up as profitability declined, this created the foundations of the future decline and eventual dissolution of the YFSR. This happened, as some theorize because of the workers not feeling as involved in the daily running of their enterprises as they did not own them, they could perform lower, reduce the profitability of their enterprises, the government would support them with subsidies and prevent their firing, those workers who owned their enterprises have a record of performing better than merely those who run them, especially if market forces are not involved.

Within the Warsaw Pact, there were similar experiments, when there was Liberalization, such as in Hungary (even after Nagy's execution), Goulash Communism, Poland, Czechoslovakia, etc. One such example, is the agricultural cooperative, JZD Slusovice in the Czechoslovakian Socialist Republic, who had a good director, some would say or a corrupt one according to others, Frantisek Cuba, showed much success during the Communist Era, although worker-ownership was not as prominent in this enterprise, Frantisek knew how to motivate people really well, with his various motivators of man, Joy from Work, Existential Fear, etc. Workers felt more involved due to him to, boosting output and productivity, a few such enterprises with hands on Directors were present in Russia too, which persevered into the Post-Cold War Era for sometime, like Nikolai Tonkov and the Tyre factory which he directed in the late '90s in Yaroslavl and another agri-cooperative that I had heard of who also had a good director (but I am forgetting his name and where he was from), these Russian directors of the quasi-coops (as I like to call them) along with their wages they also provided, hospitals, spas (important for Russians, because of their social value), pensions, housing, food, etc. all the things that were needed for good Russian life and life in general.

In the People's Republic of China, till 1976 there was much the same of the command economy shared with Russia, however at its start, agri-coops could trade in a market-like system, a part of their surplus could be sold for profit, there was also some other forms of decentralization and local rule, as the Chinese focused on the Peasants as their revolutionary base, whereas the Russians focused on the industrial workers. It is also the case that China wanted to keep what they called the Nationalist Bourgeoise on their side, that is the Capitalist who were pro-China, or pro-CCP, however, I don't know how true this is, in the sense that while Mao expressed this view, I'm sure many National Bourgeoise were lost in the Cultural Revolution and the Great Leap Forward. Even so, it is possible that amongst those who survived, their experience with Capitals, Markets and management must've allowed what trading existed on a personal or private basis to evolve into the Market-based reforms which China underwent, i.e. smoothed them Some speculate, that it is this important difference which allowed China to undergo successful market reforms as opposed to Russia, it could also be that the Chinese state was more obedient to Mao's Successors than the Russian state was to Stalin's successors. However, I do find this explanation dubious, as the Soviet Union implemented Glasnost and then subsequently collapsed a few short years after, breaking open copious amounts of classified Soviet documents, allowing us to judge the volatility of the final 4 years of the Soviet Union from 1987–1991, no such grand opening or even loosening happened for the PRC, so we can't really say what happened. India's GDP was ahead of China's till the mid-90's, so, it is entirely possible that some failures were present that were suppressed and that we are unaware of.

In Chile, there was the experiment with a similar socialist internet which wanted to coordinate production, it was of the name Cybersyn, while removed by the Pinochet government and his economic advisors of the Austrian School or the "Chicago Boys". And while it was rejected and abolished and dismantled, the Stock Market, it was eventually parallelly imitated by a capitalist and individualist version of such a system, known, as you guessed it, the stock market, it also coordinates production by taking information from as many companies as listed on it. Although Cybersyn took information of raw materials, personnel, raw output, etc. along with other metrics. The latter are metrics generally excluded from Capitalist coordination.

In Vietnam too, we know of Central-Planning modified by market-based reforms, while Cambodia's Ultra-Communism was eventually wholly rejected for State Capitalism, or State Controlled and Directed Capitalism.

Nazi Germany, while it had a centrally-planned economy which coexisted with private capital, also controlled worker's wages by encouraging them to save, which also helped fund the war, much like how the MEFO Bills helped earlier. The Germans at that time also had the necessity of keeping prices, consumption and production in check while the war was going on to prevent shortages in the war economy, this of course, led to shortages in the civilian economy and rationing.

North Korea, while still a rigid, Stalinist regime, the famine and the collapse of the Eastern Bloc, with the Liberalization of China, led to the failures of the NK economy becoming painfully evident, market- based reforms allowed much food production to become quietly privatized, even if under constant scrutiny of the state, the trade of consumer goods from China to NK, the establishment of a small middle-class, the quiet entrepreneurship and business ownership in NK, the "Socialist Enterprise Responsibility Management System (SERMS)", which devolved decision making to enterprises and allowed the sale of some surplus on a "market", even if under the scrutiny of the state, etc. even if these reforms have been recently rolled back under the new recentralization under Kim Jong-Un, during and post-covid, the state still requires greater funds, so, it is likely the bigger, more closely aligned pseudo or quasi-privatized enterprises continue to create a revenue stream for the state and acquire the smaller ones when they fail or are under pressure from the state. Not to mention that scholars of the Kim Il- Sung University, discuss and renounce SERMS, market reforms, efficiency, acceleration, reconsidering Songun (military first policy) as and when the poltical wind vane moves from favourable to unfavourable.

In India, while we had import-substitution industrialization, quasi-central planning, import tarrifs, serious regulation of the market, high bureaucracy, high taxes, etc. we also had a flourishing, semi- feudal economy (reformed partly by the Bhoodan, or voluntary land transfer movement), capitalism, market socialism through cooperatives all coexisting in our so-called state directed top-down socialism. As there was never the widespread violence and destruction of the communist revolutions of China and Russia, ours was a "peacefully" placed central-planning system which did not require the entire country to conform to these State Socialist requirements, as we had plenty of black markets, small to medium and even large private actors, village economy, personal consumption, etc.

I could go on and on about various central-planning examples and experiments, but what I think would be the ideal scenario in a Long Future, millions of years from now, would be that a Centrally-Planned system, which is cybernetic, that is like Cybersyn and OGAS, it takes in a lot of information and with decentralized central-planning, allows the coordination of goods, resources, manpower to make basic goods and services necessary for life highly affordable or even free. Working off of the psychological benefit of working for the collective and getting things done. If people sacrifice for capitalism, due to cultural values, they could do the same thing for central-planning for their fellow man. The rest of the economy, through indefinite perpetual bonds, socialization bonds, could be bought from the private sector, to ease the transition, and given to worker ownership, workers are likely to manage their enterprises better if they own them, rather than simply manage them, as they will be less likely to give a lot of pay rises to them, if the success or failure of their enterprise depends on them. This doesn't mean of course that the government won't bail out or ease the collapse of corporations in the economy, just because they're worker-managed now. Or that subsidies would disappear, it's just that now, because workers own their enterprises, and have decentralized their own enterprises, much like Haier in the PRC, the government can reduce expenditures and regulations (bureaucracy) to focus on more important matters of development.

A part cybernetically decentralized centrally-planned (with the ability to sell surplus as determined by the workers and required by the state, perhaps a middle ground between directive and indicative planning) and rest worker-owned economy with a reasonable private sector as needed, that is a truly mixed economy, would benefit the nation and its people, and prevent runaway inflation, by giving much of the economy a floor and a ceiling. In such a system, which would be oriented towards the workers and the civilian economy, the risk of shortages in the civilian economy would be limited mitigated. By borrowing from the best aspects of different Central-Planning experiments, and rejecting the bad ones, we can have an economic system that moves stably in a range while allowing for dynamism and welfare for all citizens.

Examples of what could be accommodated in this system include beyond what was mentioned above, a stock market (except with more information, like the ones socially important in Cybersyn, which would also be present in the information gathered in an encrypted fashion from all enterprises and individuals and individual businesses who wish to participate in the Department of Planning) and any other economic attribute which may not typically align with a stereotypical and orthodox planning system.

In fact, such a system should be implemented at the soonest.

How To Make Science Better

Science Unbound

Opinion Piece

Science is often in our society upheld as a neutral and objective best.

However, it was only in the 1970s that the assumption that parents could not abuse their children was overturned, which was what could be said was a conservative opinion, or that recently, the entire link between biological sex and gender is being negated, which could be considered an aspect of Liberalism, or that in the Soviet Union, it was assumed that under Lysenkoism, that crops could grow through the sheer strength of Communism, requiring nothing else, leading to wasteful if not famine inducing practices (those may have been separate), stop me if you've heard this before, the objective statement that markets will solve everything, or even if they don't, they're preferable to the alternatives, or the assumption among many scientists that no UFO can represent non-human intelligence, even though highly-strange and well-documented cases like the Japan Cargo Flight 1628 (as examined by Daniel Coumbe) show characteristics that are not defined in our standard frame of reference of =/-

10 Gs or impossible for human biology at the higher ends of the spectrum of acceleration or apparent acceleration (I say apparent, because it may that these craft are traversing wormholes, distorting gravity or doing something else instead of accelerating), or the case of the Hessdalen Lights in Norway, which inspite of continuous examination over decades, no explanation has come about to explain all sightings, at all times, from all observers, which is what science as we practice it strives for, general theories.

When it comes to Social Psychology, for decades mainstream academia did not recognize Left-Wing Authoritarianism in an empirical, testable form till the late 2010s, their main focus had been on Right- Wing Authoritarianism, even though LWA had been known for a longtime.

Isaac Newton believed in the mind of God or God, much like Einstein (even if euphemistacally), whereas today scientists believe dogmatically in the absence of God, even though that God can be testable according to science, if we our willing to make some adjustments in definition from both sides of the divide. Yes, there are religious, theistic and agnostic scientists, yet they are not as outspoken or well-known as the militant atheist group, a notable exception is Carl Sagan, who kept a more open mind.

Neutral Monism postulates that there's a neutral substrate from which both materialism and idealism are sprouts of, what is to stop this neutral substrate, from being a vast and expansive, transfinite, panentheistic God or Deity? As seen earlier in my writings, is it so impossible to measure God, whether as a blackhole, or as an entity whose effects while seemingly paranormal, may normalize to some extent, if our definitions are more flexible, such as God starting evolution, or one day in God's realm is a billion years on Earth, etc. requiring a flexibility not captured by either side's dogmatists?

This list is quite long, and I could go on forever, but if true inquiry is to prevail in the sciences, then science must be unshackled from both philosophical materialism and idealism, allowing it to ask expansive and vast questions and try to measure or experiment them, where even failure would lead to some new path or question unseen.

I am not retained by the scientific community to do their heavy lifting for them, much in the spirit of Sherlock Holmes, who is not retained by the police to solve their crimes in every situation.

Hopefully, one day an unmoored science like in Newton's or Einstein's time, will allow us to break new ground and experience the verboten.

Till then, we'll have to wait and watch.

How To Troll Daesh

A Great Way To Troll Terrorist Groups

Opinion Piece

I use the Arabic term Daesh, instead of ISIS, since ISIS was a great Ancient Egyptian Goddess, and why should disgrace her name so shamelessly by popularizing it as a term for that terrorist group?

Indeed, terrorist groups enjoy fame or infame, they like to declare themselves as the perpetrators of great violence and destruction for whatever righteous cause.

However, if there's one thing that can be learned from the Daesh attack in Moscow, and the wider Russo-Ukrainian War is that by denying them visibility and recognition, you can really piss them off, or watch them humourously clamour for attention, when denied.

What can be better for comedy than watching hardened killers whine like children when denied their prize?

In fact, even if it is for the wrong reasons, that Russia blamed the West and Ukraine for the attack, even though they were allegedly forewarned by the CIA (the masters of telling it like it is, you know), we should take away from this, that the best way to deny Daesh fame, is to just ignore them or pin their actions on someone else, indeed.

Is Clothing Immoral?

Hold On To Your Underwear!

Semi-Satirical Opinion Piece

If we were all born naked, and even as most religions put it, God made us naked, until we were later clothed, does this make clothing immoral?

To extend this further, unless we were to make the clothing ourselves, is someone else's hands always touching us? Since most clothing is made by others.

Of course, I joke, since we need clothes to protect and decorate ourselves, but it does make you wonder, if we all made our rat-fatti (raggedy) clothes, wouldn't the world be a much more interesting and hotch-potch place, then all the symmetric and pretty clothes we wear today. A specially made and skilled item of wear, would regain the legendary status it had in the past, what a beautiful romantic gesture! :)

Marriage Is A Racket

For Honourable Men

Anecdotal And Opinion Piece

In the early 20th century, a former World War 1 British soldier by the name of Smedley Butler, wrote the book, "War Is A Racket", profiteering war companies thrived on the misery and decrepitude of Europe during the first (and the second world war). However, governments are just as equally to blame, 'specially the German government, for starting the whole damn thing.

In this article, what I wish to make the case for is that, for honourable men, and before you scoff, there are plenty such men, much like the aphorism, that if there was more bad in the world than good, there would be no children born, no homes built, no nations in existence, the quiet good that goes on in every household in the land is the shining example of this goodness, for if evil was predominant, then the world would've ended. People think that war and genocide is bad, and indeed they are, however if we were not appalled by them and everyone thought like the worst concentration camp supervisor or so on, then the planet as we know would've been nasty, brutish and short.

Similarly, good, honourable men, for them marriage is a racket. I will not cover women, because they have been covered enough in that sense (and in other issues, domestic violence, dowry deaths, etc. even if domestic violence is a condition from which men also suffer, even if less).

Why is marriage a racket for the honourable man?

By law a man is required to give half his wealth to his former wife in most jurisdictions, if not more, women have the preference for custody and many children have an innate desire to be with their mother too. If the woman chooses to divorce the man, she can also assassinate the character of the man in the family, whether the wife's family and/or the husband's family.

Which of us would turn away from the plaint of a woman? Very few. It is easy to believe that the man is the evil one.

However, an honourable man, and there are many, would likely take this slight in his stride, even he resists it.

There may be accusations and opprobrium which the man faces from his own children. Even if the man may have put great emotional value and depth into his bond with his children, perhaps there is something biological in the bond for the mother, which only great stressors can remove, or the mother is beneficient, consistently or selectively.

Yes love, respect and understanding whether expansive or limited is also possible from his ex-wife and children, but, can love fully remove the trouble of the past? Maybe it can, maybe it can't.

In an ideal world, an honourable man and woman, whether in an arranged/love/live-in relationship would divide the effort mutually and not eye each other's wealth or income, they would divide or disinherit each other's wealth, rejecting the transactional aspect of the relationship as much as possible, for a more noble union. That is my dream and my hope.

Make the tough, unpalatable choices now, to prevent misery in the future.

On The Importance Of Original Meaning In Politics

Meaningful Meaninglessness

Oftentimes in politics words lose their meaning. It is advisable to keep the original meaning of words in mind to avoid being duped.

A helpful guide would be the following:

1. National Socialism: In its Pre-Nazi meaning is what passes for left-wing nationalism, or an economically left-wing National Conservatism today. The Nazis as with many other words and symbols, co-opted them to suit their purpose. You can see this word being used in its original meaning in the Czech Republic, by the Czech National Social Party and its breakaways, or the National Socialist Council of Nagaland and its many factions in India. While it causes much angst to socialists as it originally had nothing to do with Nazism, as we know in politics, the cynic, the extremist, the ardent believer will use the most tenuous of links to denounce something, however that is not a reason to shy away from it. 😊 Perhaps one day, the socialists will get over their fear, anger and anxiety and reappropriate the word, but I doubt it. Not to mention how the Swastika has been a symbol for

peace and harmony for thousands of years prior to Nazi Germany, the best way to get rid of its potency with the Nazi cause, would be to celebrate it in its original form and meaning. But good luck with that outside of Asia.

2. Libertarian: Before the 1950s, the word Libertarian meant what today is the Socialist Anarchist School. This term was co-opted by the adherents of a very particular strand of the Monetarist School, who were also a very particular brand of free-market anti-statist capitalists, calling themselves the Austrian School. One should enjoy wonderful snippets of joyful Freedom from the likes of Rothbard and Hayek, where he said, "Thus, Rothbard stated that parents should have the legal right to let any infant die by starvation and should be free to engage in other forms of child neglect. However, according to Rothbard, 'the purely free society will have a flourishing free market in children'. I'd like to remind you that a wonderful and probably very free market in children in the form of food, porn and sex already exists, it's just illegal, and some of it is in North Korea. :D From Hayek we have the excellent insight that people have socialistic tendencies from birth and these need to be removed. A true champion of natural rights and freedoms. 😊 Anyways, this is one more chance for socialists to reappropriate "Libertarian", but doubtful it will happen. They should get Stalinists and Leninists to reply for them by embracing the baby murder and eating of Stalinist and Leninist famines,

it'll be a glorious world when these two very particular ideologues can see eye to eye. 😊

3. Liberalism: This word meant free-markets and limited government, when it was classical liberalism, but like Fascism, Nazism, Socialism and Communism has lost its original meaning to just mean different flavours of Modern Day Progressivism. We should ask American Libertarians to start calling themselves Liberals again, just so that the United States (US) Republican Party can excommunicate them when they say "Economic Liberalism" :D

4. Conservatism: Just like all the other words above, we should put Conservatism to rest, as its original meanings of either Maistre's Theocracy or Burke's Ordered Liberty centred on the community has morphed into anywhere from Ayatollah Ali Khomenei's Ultraconservatism, to Conservatives who blush when they're called Socialist and prefer the term "paternalistic" and to people just short of Fascism or Nazism or like the "Libertarians" above, who are "socially conservative", but there's no plan on how without a state any doggone conservatism will happen. :D

I didn't mention the usual suspects of milquetoast Socialism, Communism, Fascism or Nazism, because these have been covered Ad Nauseam before, and can serve no more purpose. Now we have new words to add to the bin of history. :D

Paradoxes In Capitalism: Choice And Efficiency

What is Capitalism If Choice And Efficiency Fail?

Questioning Piece TLDR:

Less choice would be more efficient, but less choice is anti-capitalist in a way. More choice is less efficient, but is more consistently capitalist.

Linkages: Time Efficiency vs Dual Choice, Production Efficiency vs Allocation Efficiency (areas of conflict)

xxxxxxxxxxxxxx Definitions

Production Efficiency: More goods for lower cost (cheap and large quantity), superproduction, superabdundance, streamlined production around a limited number of products or product, much like a startup, but on a more macroscale.

Allocation Efficiency: Efficiency in the distribution of goods.

Time Efficiency: Acting on prior bias or choices to speed up a decision, while rejecting choices without examining them or being educated about the products, in a way reducing choices for decision-making efficiency.

"Dual" Choice: What to produce and what to buy. Examples:

1. Mcdonnell Douglas, the US aircraft manufacturer, produced the DC-9 before the highly successful variant, the MD-80. These losses lead to the eventual merger between Douglas and McDonnell to create the new company.

2. Tata Nano in India. A car by Tata for India's poor, which went through a tortuous production cycle for over a decade with much invested in it, factories, workers, land, etc. The poor chose higher cost cars due to the social value attached to them. Or bought bikes or scooters if they were too poor. They ended up selling about 200–300,000 vehicles. It was a capable car, much like the sufficiently capable DC-9 as mentioned above, but for the aforementioned reasons, the car did not sell with a success which matched the success of the design (eventually).

3. When goods get ultra-cheap, then destroying, burying or dumping the goods is more affordable than transporting or selling the goods without government support through either minimum support prices or by facilitation through transport subsidies or direct intervention or at the personal expense of the producer. If the removal of the circulation of the goods is the solution that the "market" reaches, then it goes against distributing the cheapest goods on the market.

This is a comparison within Capitalism and not to say that Socialism is better or worse.

xxxxxxxxxxxxxxxxx

Conundrum

In many interpretations of Capitalism, choice and efficiency are central covenants to capitalist economic thought.

However, too much choice, or even many choices can lead to inaction or inefficiency (making the same thing over and over again with only minor differences). I don't mean Venture Capitalists acting as gatekeepers of similar ideas or even new ideas which they think are unviable for investment, I mean established companies producing within or without (intracompany and intercompany), very similar or not largely meaningfully different products. This is not a comment on their sales or their attraction by customers, it's a more fundamental question of reconciling the paradox of choice (i.e. with itself) and the problem that arises when a sub-optimal number of choices reduce efficiency. Many inefficient companies chug along and unproductive product chains continue, so more exploratory answers than, "the company collapses" or they "change the product line" would be appreciated.

xxxxxxxxxxxxxxxxx

Query

Would these conflicts exist under Socialism, if not, then why not?

How would socialism solve them? Hyperinflation from money printing to destroy the value of money, focus on aggregate output instead of relative output, a new equilibrium through a worker-managed market, something else?

Paradoxes In Communism:Revolution

When Your Revolution Leads Back To What You Sought To Remove. Ouroboros.

Opinion Piece

The most common interpretation of Communism is Marxist Communism and its derivatives as opposed to Religious Communism or Anarchist Communism, or any other kind of Communism (such as pre- agricultural Communism, to whatever extent it existed, supposedly, congruent with Marx's term, "Primitive Communism").

Marx understood eventually that Capitalism would not necessarily collapse, as it could always renew itself, hence, requiring a revolution to bring about Communism through the state in his view. This revolution was meant to emancipate the worker from the exploitation of Capitalism, and lead to the establishment of a classless, moneyless, stateless society. Anarcho-Communists jumped over this step, to say that the revolution should immediately establish this reality. Whether or not you agree or disagree, is not something which we will get into here.

However, such a revolution could only happen in Marx's view after Capitalism had fully developed, and not in agricultural societies like Tsarist Russia or Republican China. What fully developed looks like is anyone's guess, but it is likely a stage just before post-scarcity, which would theoretically render conversations of Capitalism and Communism, mute. Although rent-seeking and ownership structures would still determine whether it were a Capitalist or a Socialist form of Post-Scarcity. The one who has the penny which could buy anything would be on top, or owned the replicators, or any other magical device. If deflation or hyperdeflation set in, it likely would lead to a Depression unlike any before, as people would wait till prices were near zero, less than the 1/100th of currency, to purchase large quantities of goods (theoretically, people would still buy things, as humans are not pure rational economic agents).

Marx then differentiated between Socialism, or the Lower Stage of Communism and the Upper Stage of Communism, or Communism Communism (Pure Communism).

In implementing Marx's ideas, and I won't get into the critique of implementing his ideas in a peasant- dominant society, lets just say that the Capitalism in Post-Tsarist Russia during the Russian Civil War for the sake of our argument, was just about as far as you were going to get, due to the historical happenings at that time, the fallout from WW1. This was as good as Capitalism was going to get in early 20th Century Russia.

The Paradox then arises that, in devaluing money to the point of near nothingness with stratospheric hyperinflation (money is capital after all, even if it is "revolutionary money" which is not meant to be neutral), in the practice of War Communism, in the beggaring of the countryside, where catastrophic famine was stopped only by the intervention of the United States, where industrial capacity of Russia was only at 13 to 25% of the pre-war total (depending on which document you read), where all opponents to Pure Communism atleast in the Marxian, or Marxist-Leninist sense had been swept away in 1923 (for the most part), then what was the need to bring back Capitalism?

War Communism had already weakened the peasants compared to the urban worker, the famine was being resolved by help of the United States (regardless of whether you differ on the interpretation of their motives), the entire industry which remained had been almost entirely retooled towards war production, the experienced Soviet Army had been great in size and strength just after the Russian Civil War, if not with the best weaponry, the airforce had just been formed, the Navy was mostly intact, the rolling stock, while damaged heavily, could easily have been repaired with the help of the Americans, much like Stalin did later with Collectivization, Industrialization and Grain Exports for Capital Goods, technology and know-how, the bedrock of Capitalism had been destroyed by the abolition of private property and the steep devaluation of money, private enterprise except for the bagmen who carried food from the countryside to the cities and what black markets that managed to function, were all that remained of Capitalism as the rest of the industry and property and economy in the nation had been nationalized and I could go on and on. For all intents and purposes Communism had been achieved as best as could be after two devastating wars and just about as far as Capitalism could've gotten in Feudal Russia for the foreseeable future (as even if Tsarist Russia had survived, demobilization and retooling to civilian industry and lowering of taxes and levies would likely have led to Depression).

Perhaps the Bolsheviks were motivated by ideology to carry through Marx's historical materialism, perhaps they were surprised at the quickness of the establishment of Communism in Feudal Russia, without the need of "Fully Developed Capitalism", maybe it was something else, who really knows?

But the point, that is, what the nature of the paradox is, is that the revolution created the perfect conditions for Capitalism to come roaring back if just given the chance, which is what it was given for a good 5–6 years under the NEP, or the New Economic Program (essentially revitalized capitalism, existing outside the commanding heights of the economy).

Stalin showed that even in its denoued state, the Soviet Union could embark on a crash industrialization and modernization program, as I find it unlikely that the damage of those nine years from 1914 to 1923 (and in some places till 1926) could be undone in just 5 to 6 short years, even if the revitalized capitalism brought back some life to the economy and gave the party some breathing space, especially with the people of the Soviet Union.

My point is that the destruction caused from total uncompromizing revolution, leads to the paucity of Capital in an economy, which, if central planning and mass mobilization is not utilized to overcome, then leads to the conditions which revives Capitalism back from the dead, throwing a spanner into the works of Marxist Communism, atleast in the way that it has been implemented in the real world.

Communist China while less total in its transition to Communism, while maintaining some markets and co-ops (such as in farming), also saw widespread famine and cultural decline, which could be called "Communist Shock Therapy", when a traditional, agricultural, guild-based and market-oriented economy is subjected to shock which converts it into a totalitarian communist state (unlike Pure Marxism). This, you can be much obliged to think, is the inverse of "Capitalist Shock Therapy", which usually does the opposite, but generally without the traditionalism, guilds, agrarianism, etc.

It's quite possible that there are Marxists who do realize this paradox, especially if they advocate for revolution before the full development of capitalism, or worker's rights, or welfare, etc. which prevents the contradictions of capitalism from collapsing itself (out of fear or concern of what they define as Fascism).

Those Marxists who do recognize this, probably support Market Socialism, through various kinds of Co-Ops, as according to Marx in Capital Volume 3, both co-ops and stock markets represent an improvement over earlier forms of Capitalism. One can think of them as the moderates in the Marxist movement, who want a transition away from Capitalism, one based in worker ownership of the means of production, without necessarily the full force of the state behind it (it being relegated to a more supportive role to establish this Market Socialism), with a bottom-up movement, more akin to Anarchist forms of Socialism and Marxism.

As long as Capital exists, and the recognition of nature in such terms, Capitalism will too, in some form, even if illegal, ignored, repressed and diminished.

Most intriguing indeed.

Paradoxes In Conservatism:History

Life Is Paradoxical, So Is ideology

Opinion Piece

Lest it seem that I am committed to only finding Paradoxes in Liberalism and the Left, even if in my belief and view, my articles are more even-keeled, conservatism too, due to its storied past and its vast scope and difference from region to region and time to time, has its fair share of paradoxes, although perhaps less egregious and hidden or ignored than those in Liberalism, albeit that too depends on who is looking and where.

In nations with unconquered pasts like the United Kingdom or the United States (who successfully and early on overthrew its overlord, and whose overload was culturally quite similar, that is why Burke saw American Revolution evolutionary rather than revolutionary like that of the French, as he saw it as limited and justified, based upon the right of the ruled to overthrow the ruler on the basis of him overstepping his governing boundaries, while that was present among the French too, they resorted to widespread violence and a more systemic and broad restructuring of society, removing the church, expanding the franchise, etc. let us also ignore the later reinstatement of the monarchical but less absolute rule under Napoleon, which probably did more to dismantle the monarchy, due to its failures in the Napoleonic Wars than the revolution itself, as the Napoleonic Wars failed utterly, as opposed to bitterness which the revolution inspired from its excesses), the past is hallowed ground where the dominant culture did no wrong, where the preservation of past can be absolute, unrivalled, progressive, civilizing, etc. They oppose the removal of monuments of this mythical and great past, the demonization of Anglo-Saxon culture, religion, beliefs and so on. The might of past nation builders, where those who were crushed or brushed aside can be easily ignored under manifest destiny or paternalistic compassion and various other nation building and national stories, these, while contested can still be told with pride, due to the unbrokenness that these represent.

But, in conquered countries, the relation with the past for the conservatives is more complicated, where, like Russia (not conquered but with a revolutionary history) and other Nations like India, have to pick and choose which parts of history to showcase and be triumphalist about.

The Pre-Vedic period till the first sultanate in India during the 11th century can be seen as an unbroken cord of Indian history for conservatives. After which there is a long Muslim rule till the British rule. Where the focus on Muslim rule, even if different in its nature and duration and dynasties and barbarity or softness to Hindus, etc. can be lumped together for simplicity in rhetoric and storytelling as it is the longest foreign occupation of India.

Of course, an easy answer for those who question why when Indian Kings and Emperors could be just as merciless and brutal, there's the focus on outsiders, the answer is that people hate a foreign invasion much more than that of somebody who talks, dresses and thinks like you, almost exclusively.

Foreign invasions also unite all disparate forces in a nation in due time, even if after the invaders have been defeated the warring factions go back to their internecine quarrels. Those foreign rulers with staying power have to balance internal factions, external factions, outside pressures, mixing brutality with fair governance and compassion, etc. it keeps people fearful but also gracious, and likely would be no different from what Chanakya and Machiavelli would prescribe to a ruler, to mix fear with love, worship with hatred, compassion with brutality, etc. or what is known as political pragmatism, realism, cynicism, etc. these are not perfect solutions to governance, in the least bit, but they keep subject populations guessing about your very next move and what they should or can do, without attracting your wrath and only your beneficence. While this is a laudable but questionable approach to governance, Indian conservatives would likely create a national narrative which undermines Muslim rule in India, due to its length and distance from the Indian present, while keeping conversations about the British Raj more muted, as we see today.

That is also because we need the foreign capital and expertise and the bandwagon of the West as opposed to the Muslim nations for our countering of China, creating of our internal myth and the economic advancement of our country, hence, the more muted critique of our former western colonial masters, the duration of Western rule was also shorter, which helps in some small part.

However the paradox arises when many among the more radical among the conservatives and traditionalists, while perhaps in many cases recognizing the need for quietitude about the British, whether for their outsize influence, reach and power, or for the fact that by the fear of losing their place among their less radical brethren, other traditionalists and conservatives try to restrict or marginalize them, their target becomes the Era of Muslim rule, renaming roads, demonizing that period selectively or in total, etc.

While I haven't seen extend as far as the removal and vandalization of old monuments by the members of the progressives and liberals in the West, these I'm sure can happen among the conservatives too, one need only look at the Revisionism of Hitler (although he stands out among the rest, in wanting to destroy and embrace the past, Mussolini in comparison intended to preserve history more, desirous to bring back the Roman Empire, which led to his quite heavy-handedness about it and in the end caused its demise in a way, one could say by his very extremism). One can look at it as not paradoxical, as it is something foreign or alien to the culture with which it happened, however, by erasing this history for radical conservatives, or wanting to incorporate it into the present for moderate conservatives, then it creates in the first case, the incontinuity with the past that many conservatives despise, and in the second case, trying to fit a square peg into a round hole, and attempting to fit the alien culture into the present. With Liberal Universalism, this is less of a problem, as Liberals want greater intermixing and integration even between former adversaries (which can create its own contradictions and fuel for conservatism). Many Constitutions are Liberal and foist themselves on mostly or exclusively conservative populations. This creates plenty of friction in society, lest we forget that in the agricultural period of the World, monarchies have existed for far longer than democracies, this may not ascribe to their success, but uniting behind the divinity or absolute power of one leader, does do away with the messiness and divergent pulls within democracy, whether or not we like it. If this is something that will repeat in the future remains to be seen.

One way out for from this catch-22, is to build upon the advancements in each age by recognizing the contributions of each Era without overexultation or overcriticism, and then using traditional knowledge mixed with modernity to create a uniquely "own-cultural" solution to problems. It can be as simple as examining the aerodynamics of the Pushpak Vimaans in India and the promotion of Unani and Ayurved or in its more intense avtaar, the usage of direct Vedic, or Pre-Vedic or Post-Vedic but pre-Islamic knowledge to arrive at solutions to pressing modern problems. Such as using the Arthshastr to organize society from the bottom-up. That might be a way to resolve the paradox, and it remains to be seen whether conservatives can manage it successfully, without twisting themselves into knots like our Russian Conservative friends have, by trying to reconcile Tsarist and Soviet Histories into One, Indivisible, United Russia.

Paradoxes In Ideology: A Matter of Nature And Purpose

Ideology Poses A Threat To Itself

Opinion Piece

It is evident from my "Paradoxes In X" series, ideologies have paradoxical natures detrimental to their continuance, either it creates scenarios where people revolt, like Feudalism, where people do not wish to isolationist, as in Ultra-Traditionalism (but this is compensated by population growth), the destruction of future growth through abortion in Liberalism, majority of Leftist, some types of Conservatism (especially the Eastern types), etc.

The self-contradictory, moreso, those which are much more potent which lead to self-decline, are emblematic of internal or external factors which naturally decline ideologies, their groups and lead to social change and upheaval.

While this may seem biased, the fact remains that traditionalism leads to the most guaranteed and sustainable population growth after Feudalism, but with it comes its own problems of stagnation.

In Capitalism there is a tension between choice and efficiency, in socialism between individual freedoms and collective goods, in Fascism, the use of state power instead of personal power, in communism, the paradox of revolutions negating themselves, and so on and so forth.

Every ideology has self-contradictory elements which threaten its own survival, even if we ignore the criticisms from outside about various negative aspects of them.

Paradoxes In Liberalism: Age of Legal Sex

Also Known As The Age Of Consent

Opinion Piece

There is a perception about Liberalism in general and specific to the Anglo-Saxon West and the English speaking Liberals of India and the rest of South Asia, that increased age of consent laws are a sign of progress. However, I am here to show that even when we exclude Libertarians, it is possible for Liberals to come around to a reduced age of consent.

In the past, there were many discussions between Liberals and Traditionalists, about where the age-of- consent should lie, and how much higher it should be. Many traditionalists were also onboard with this idea, wanting progress in their own communities. Child marraiges could happen as young as nine, and be consummated soon, if puberty was early-onset, although usually by 13 and 14. Infant marraiges were not consummated legally for obvious reasons.

In India, during its formation, the age agreed was 16 and then eventually rose to 18 and even 21 for men. In the Anglo-Saxon world, save for a few exceptions about 15 and 16, the age eventually increased to 18, legislatures requiring a cutoff point for adulthood for governing, legal and bureaucratic purposes (even if the brain doesn't fully mature till the age of 25–26, the age when the plasticity of the brain starts to decline almost exclusively).

But as you can see once progress has been achieved and a certain gender parity is available, countries considered at the forefront of this change like Iceland, dropped their age of consent gradually to 15. Bringing us back to the vicinity of ultra-traditional age numbers, or even those who advocate more strongly for it, like the Libertarians (keeping to its recent free-market, anti-statist and capitalist connotations in many Anglo-Saxon and its cultural offshoot parts of the World).

What this implies is that once the equality is reached, magically the oppressive rule or power imbalance of youth marriage is removed as the Liberals would define it. Now leaving individuals free-to-choose, once this magical state has been reached. Atomized and highly individualized people at these ages, impressionable, young, full of excitement and a desire for experiences, may find these relations good or bad, however they may lack the support systems in traditional marraige structures which were in place for child marraiges, leaving people worse off than before. Granted many Liberals do oppose this, but there's no guarantee that these changes won't happen in the future, if Liberalism in that country continues to strongly persist.

This brings me back to what I've always wondered, the blind faith of Liberalism in individual choice, even if they say that individuals are not perfect and they can or should make mistakes, the philosophy itself rests on the primacy of individual choices. Granted community choices or government choices may not be the best either, but atleast they involve a support system. Critics may counter that in Liberalism, atleast people can choose their support system, but people self-sort and assuming that their support system is based off similarly highly individualized people, is there any guarantee of sustained or appropriate support? Requiring professional help (which to be frank after having experienced it for quite some time, I am quite skeptical of it). Are these the self-sustaining, self-sufficient rational economic agents of Liberalism?

Those lucky few who are so able to stand on their feet in all or most things, are likely surivivalists, who anyways don't fit the mould of most forms of Liberalism, so, I cannot say what pragmatic outcomes can be expected from Liberalism, perhaps it will like other systems in the past, continue till it cannot continue any further.

Paradoxes In Pornography And Hard Drugs: Consumer Degradation

When Your Industry Cannabilizes Itself

Opinion Piece

Hard Drugs And Related Substances

As drug gangs across the world, but 'specially in the US, Central America, South America, are finding out that drugs like Fentanyl, Krokodil and other drugs which are incredibly easy to overdose on and kill their consumer base, they are themselves taking proactive action to limit the spread of these very drugs. You find the grim hilarity of hardened drug gangs running rehab clinics, trying to wean off the very people they spent years getting hooked on their products. This puts them into conflict with those gangs who, usually younger, are not concerned or think that such trivialities will not affect them. Of course, as with any bubble, the reality is inescapable, the further that the hardest drugs permeate society and replace those which people are used to earlier (Heroin and Cocaine, while dangerous, are nowhere near the poisonous power of Fentanyl and Krokodil). Something even as seemingly innocuous as DNP, the weight loss steroid, can be easily overdosed on and cause death. Which only uptil a few years ago, you could easily get on Google or on ecommerce sites.

What this eventually results in, that as governments grow in power and strength as time passes on, something which generally happens, as governments get better at governing over time, this will mean that the drug dealing industry (i.e. hard drugs, just to clarify, not soft drugs or medicinal drugs, although they have their own recorded problems), will over time, as it is unable to get new adherents (purposely used, as many find an inescapable bond to drug use), what this will lead to is the eventual self-implosion of hard drugs, till it is a minimal or non-existent part of society.

Pornography (mostly hardcore)

Besides the usual moral opposition to pornography, especially hardcore pornography and the commonly understood problems of erectile dysfunction, sexual anhedonia (pleasurelessness, lack of pleasure), romantic lapse, relational issues, abnormal sexual expectations, unrealisitc sexual expectations (pornstars usually boast staminas, physiques, secondary sexual characteristics, sociosexuality and behaviours far in excess of the average human baseline, whether negative or positive), premature ejaculation, stimulation failure, risk taking to induce stimulation, etc., all these could reduce the viewership of porn in its user base, but a problem which is more real while being ironic is described below.

The real problem that lies here is that a few studies which I have read show that porn turns conservatives into liberals, at least where it comes to sex. Some conservatives, mind you, not all. Liberals generally view sex less than their conservative counterparts in the United States. Not to extrapolate on limited data, but if I can be so bold so as to state that hardcore porn, like any destructive addictive substance cannabilizes its own consumer base. Although not seen in any study by me, people could also through repulsion, disgust, guilt, anhedonia, depressed stimulant response, etc. become inured to pornography (and drugs) and leave, or also find their conservative or non-explicit views on sex reinforced (say romantic views for example) and leave porn watching.

Conservatives and traditionalists (those few traditionalists that do watch), could also use their religion in conjunction with their social circles to move out of porn viewing, through a mixture of repulsion and guilt.

Conclusion

In concluding, as demonstrated above, if the porn and drug industries don't find some way of mitigating these harmful tendencies, then they will find themselves cannibalized out of existence, by their very selves.

Perhaps for the best, leaving us with much better substitutes like erotica, sacred nudity, art and expressive stimulants of the mind done through meaningful work.

Paradoxes In Fascism: Strength

Strength for us and no one else

Opinion Piece

Fascists often talk of strength as a core virtue of their ideology/philosophy, and a few Fascists, even though their targets are at lower or equal strength, Ernst Rohm and Jose Antonio Primo De Rivera, did take personal risk when taking on their opponents and duking it out in the streets of their cities and countries, the fact of the matter is that most Fascists were content to merely use the power of the state when they got it, to remove their enemies.

This does not seem to match the superhuman strength or will, the New Man they wished to create. Certainly, a superman would be one who could defeat someone as capable and skilled as him in equal and fair combat, or even if in an unfair fight, rely on his own strength as much he could to either win, stalemate or lose in an as honourable manner as possible.

Perhaps there were some elements of stability in Austrofascism, Estado Novo (Portugal) and in the later years of Falangism (Spain), however, these regimes had their own sordid histories, but none matched the warlordism, typified by the brutality of the Nazi Regime.

How Fascists could balance righteous strength as a virtue is unknown to me, it would require a softer personality and more restraint, much like Kurt Von Schussnigg and Peron in Argentina, but then, once Fascism gets softer leaders, it eventually evolves into a democracy.

I don't personally think that this is a conundrum that Fascists can solve.

Poverty Has An Endgame

Reducing Poverty Instantaneously Without Hyperinflation or Heavy Tax Burden Or Indebting The Poor

Opinion Piece

Using the data from the website, "Our World In Data", global poverty on all poverty lines has gone down, although using the "$120" a day poverty line, poverty on a global level has barely changed. Although this makes sense, since this is nearly double the minimum wage of the United States, the richest country in the world in absolute terms.

However, some countries which have more generous minimum wages, likely make up that small change we see and the creation of the new class of wealthy and the super-wealthy and the upper-middle class.

Even so, extreme poverty is on the decline since the 18th century, around the time that the industrial revolution started.

However, to supercharge this process, what is necessary is to establish a worker's democracy. When we have worker ownership of the businesses that they used to work in, then they can partake in the process of wealth generation and profit accrual.

For those who critique this process on so-to-speak, cold, hard and efficiency based terms.

Examples where worker-owned enterprises do better is seen in Mondragon in Spain, where the locality in Spain where it is, is the richest locality in Spain.

AMUL lead the White Revolution in India, where it became the largest Milk Producer in the World thanks to AMUL.

In China there is Haier, a world-class HVAC producer and manufacturer, Semco in Brazil, which survived the hyperinflationary period of the 1990s in Brazil, is worker-managed, even if capital owned, and is one of the best export companies in Brazil, I could go on with examples, but any such critiques are purely ideological. If however people wish to genuinely engage with making WREs better that is a separate matter, there is definitely room for improvement and bringing them into advanced technology sectors and more decentralized production, such as experiments in the US and the Netherlands with modular nuclear energy generation in Universities through co-ops.

The more that co-ops are involved in high-tech sectors (and not just adopting high-tech, such as AMULs procurement of the best Swedish milk centrifuges) is an area of serious investigation and incorporation into co-ops. This would also generate more income and asset wealth for the workers and accelerate the reduction of poverty in poor nations, rather than relying solely on outmoded forms of welfare, self-help groups and other such endeavours, which are good, but are subject to the whims of unstable/highly competitive markets, government policy (welfare cuts or boosts) and lack of asset ownership, which is present in co-ops.

It also flies in the face of the cynical view that poverty will eventually fall in 2–300 years, so why accelerate the decline. Clearly this attitude is not held among the folks who hold these views when it comes to technological advancement, perhaps they have a vested stake in the advancement of tech, as it suits their selfish interests, of money and/or comforts or their own narrow goals of progress.

In due time, more workers will garner self-respect and self-advancement and the exploitative class of big capital will find that they have lost their dictatorial power over workers.

Many businesses are already worker co-ops, maybe they just go unnoticed.

ICA COOP's data (conflicting information exists from the UN, but that might be due to the sample size they chose, the study from the ILO says that a systematic and worldwide survey of all co-ops is needed to truly understand their assets, liabilities, number of workers, revenue streams and so on, while this is true for private corporations, it is even more so for co-ops, who, even though there are notable exceptions of formally accounted co-ops, are largely informal, unregistered and unlisted), if trusted, show that 33% of the global workforce was in a co-op, this does not include those firms which are Labour

Managed but Capital Owned (like Semco), which one could consider a form of economic democracy too.

(The Poor Would Also Protected From Predatory Profit-Maximizing Microfinance Companies)

Reducing Fire Danger In Nuclear Power Plants

Paratamized By The Hell Patrol

Opinion Piece

A Normobaric Hypoxic (or normal air pressure low oxygen) environment in the case of a normal fire, say a Hydrogen fire in a Nuclear Reactor Building and its surrounding areas will disallow any blaze in Nuclear Reactors from getting out of hand.

If however a nuclear incident does happen, such an environment would help protect fire fighters from radiation to an extent. I fluid environments such as air or water, hypoxia is shown to reduce the absorption of radioactive emissions. This is most evident at lower radiation doses, while at very high radiation doses, the protection imparted from hypoxia is lesser but still evident. In the event of an emergency, the environment could be made selectively hypoxic post-evacuation and that firefighters are supplied with an independent and shielded oxygen supply.

This hypoxic environment will protect the firefighters from radiation atleast to an extent, hopefully, the oxygen scrubbers would not be destroyed. For catastrophic explosions, the concrete itself could act as an absorber of Oxygen from the air, if it is specially made for this purpose.

At higher radiation doses any which ways, the emergency response would for a long time be from a distance, for the most part (with extensive protection).

This Normobaric Hypoxic environment would be recommended for low level likes or conventional fires and not for the large disruptions seen at Chernobyl, Fukushima, Kyshtym, etc.

For example, augmentations made to nuclear reactors would allow flooding the reactor with a dense and inert gas like Argon, which would flood the reactor, snuffing out any fires and providing a good barrier against fission byproducts/radiation post-evacuation (to prevent suffocation). Even in the face of catastrophic failure, which is much rarer now, due to much better and modular reactor design and protective enclosures around the fissile material, the dense Argon layer would allow atleast some protection against lethal radiation, specially to those alive closest to the core.

Modern 4th Gen and potential 5th Gen Nuclear Reactors will have extensive safety, beyond what we have today, whereas today we can have reactors controlled by students in Universities and fission moderation without water (that is the reactor does not require water to control the fission reactions), future reactors maybe small, far more modular devices enclosed with Argon gas and maybe fill up Nuclear Parks (like industrial and office parks) which provide ultra-save, decentralized, energy-dense, inexpensive, supercriticality proof and with minimal radioactive waste (using the lessons learnt from breeder reactors and others).

The safety profile of nuclear reactors is almost complete, and we are at the cusp of mass-producing safe and inexpensive nuclear energy, after many years of research and development.

Seeing Can Be Believing

Strange Tidings To You

Anecdotal Piece

The term "seeing is believing" holds true for many things, it's even important in science. However there are criticisms of it, it is prone to misreporting, memory suggestions, etc. generally the greater or more reliable number of geographically separate independent witnesses, the higher is the veracity of the claim.

In the case of viewing the divine in its many shapes or forms and UFOs, cryptids, etc., seeing is not believing atleast for skeptical scientists (as opposed to more neutral scientists, who say, "tell me why you think so") and hard skeptics, rightly or wrongly. It's not my intention to convince you of the merits of this story, but it does make me wonder.

My father's maternal grandmother or Nani in Hindi, was quite a strong believer or certainer (perhaps a better term, belief presumes that her thoughts had an element of unreality or skepticism about God).

She often used to pray to God/s, Krishna was the most prominenet among them. A Krishn Bhakt, or Krishn worshipper. Dropping the "A" to keep it closer to its original pronunciation.

On one such occasion, she said that she saw God, God came to her in her awake self and appeared right in front of her and filled her room with light.

My father recalled that when she had this vision, the intensity of light under her door was quite high, not the kind you would expect from a tubelight, it was more like as if a searchlight was on in her room, radiating an intense light under the door sill, or the gap between the bottom of the door and the floor.

One could say that it would be more believable for a UFO or Ghost or Advanced Alien to have manifested, if we were to reach for a paranormal explanation, than God himself.

However, one could ask if keeping with the paranormal explanation and solely on the basis of belief, why couldn't have she have seen God?

Is it so hard to imagine God's existence, just because it is so antithetical to a materialist and rationalist thought?

Sri Aurobindo said that for the materialist, God appears as the material world. It does make sense that God would have no limitations, and would appear in the form most comfortable to us, for the materialist, the material world, for the aformalist believer or certainer (so-to-speak), the bright white light, or a bright light, for one who believes both, a white light, or a light with God himself in a formalist form appear before the worshipper.

Could it have been any of the other paranormal things, sure, but I like to belief, nay, be certain that it was some heavenly form which apparitioned in front of my dad's Nani. After all it might explain why those who are faithless, or lost faith, do not see God or feel the warmth that pervades other believers, either God has become the material world in its entirety as cold and barren as such a world would be, except the spiritualism from beauty, aesthetics or space, as some scientists tell us, or as some who were previously faithful tell us. Or as I myself have felt. Or that God feels no need to manifest himself among those who are not worshippers, reflecting back unto them what they see.

God if all-powerful and all-knowing and all-seeing should be capable of this.

Although I don't think that God is so cold-hearted, for even those who have lost faith or are in the depths of despair, may feel the warmth of God through other avenues, hobbies/professions that they enjoy, the presence and affection of their loved ones, the solace emanating from sacred sites, etc. etc.

There are those few who even after the reversal to worship find themselves in a nearly barren desert, punctuated with oases of that divine deeling, I among them. Perhaps in due time those powerful feelings of oneness shall return, perhaps this is some test, some "time-out", maybe it is that I can't let God in fully in as before, hence, this sense of abandonment and lack of paradise.

Whatever it may be, I think that what my dad's Nani saw was the real deal, the real McCoy. Her greatness and devotion, granted her this boon, seen nary by a few in history.

It is enough for me, I suppose, I needn't see God, or have him manifest in front of me, just his divine touch on my family was enough.

I hope that if there is a reunification with the Great Soul, that will provide the much sought solace that has eluded me, and for all those that wander seemingly alone in feeling of barrenness.

Socialism Does Everything Better Than Capitalism, Even, Slavery

Everything is done better in Socialism Even Immorality

Opinion Piece

On a recent conversation with someone on Reddit, about the merits slash demerits of Capitalism versus Socialism, yes, on Reddit of all places, I am aware of your eye-rolling. :)

You know you're on the right path when communists and capitalists vehemently disagree with you.

However, to get back to the point, yes, on one such forum, we came to comparing the various things that co-ops (that is cooperatives, where the workers, producers, consumers, etc. but generally workers, own the means of production) could do versus privately owned enterprises (that is only owned by one person, or generally people who don't work there, like the private individuals who have lots of money/capital).

I gave various examples such as modular nuclear power plants (University or non-University), milk co- ops like AMUL which are very large and so on and so forth, and his argument was that private companies could do better than co-ops in every scenario, so I gave a reply that even if socialists ran a space station, he would reject that example, then he said that even if socialists ran a slave camp, I would say socialism would be better, so I gave the witty repartee, "Why YES! Socialism would do slavery better!"

It was meant to be a witty repartee, however when one thinks about it, what has the best that Slavery has done under Capitalism/Feudalism, it built the Roman Empire over a few decades and under Capitalism it had central planning in the form of Company Towns, where every store, piece of land and everything else in a designated area was owned by the concerned company, for extracting of precious goods, like Gold, Silver, Copper, Iron, Coal, etc.

Under semi-feudalism the best that was created was a series of plantations in the American South, undoutbtedly valuable, but not as much as what the Soviets did.

With Central Planning, though brutal, with the gulags and the general slave labour, Penal or otherwise, the Soviets built a country from the 13% of pre-1913 industrial output to the second-largest superpower in a matter of 25–30 years (1917–1947). However, it is also true that they brought it to that state in the first place, where its economy was beragarg or completely done for.

What this shows is that when done properly, Socialism can do great things, terrible, but great things, if an amoral or immoral form of socialism is followed.

If it had followed morally, or even if the Tsarist Regime had continued, we likely would've seen similarly rapid industrialization. What we need is Socialism with morality, then it can finally be the superior system, based on morals and spiritual growth too.

The Future Is Scientifically Racist

Buy One Get One Racism Free

Semi-Satirical Opinion Piece

We have used moral and religious arguments in the past to exculpate Racism and move ourselves forward towards a more equal era.

However, today, biology is used as a tool to discredit racism.

But if we assume that mankind expands outward to the stars or becomes biologically distinct on Earth as it was in the pastl, then one can easily imagine that when this cleavage happens, then mankind could just as easily use science to justify racism, and who are we to oppose science? Since we are different, we must be different, commence the segregation.

This could apply even to the conversations about sex change. If a person says they're something then they are, but we also use science and biology to justify such choices, which is strange, since just earlier, we couldn't use it to justify racism, until of course we become biologically distinct.

Of course, taken to its logical conclusion, hermaphroditic humans could evolve, with females that undergo self-fertilization, natural sex change and parthenogenesis, all these could be programmed into humans, if certain sub-sections of populations have cultural values which adhere to this, will we have sexual segregation based off of biological differentiation? The logical endpoint of blurring the line between the sexes. We speciate into different sexually reproductive species, where the original still remains as "rigid" as us. Well, I'm all for it, let them have internal fertilization as far as I'm concerned, much like all progress, some of us will remain boring and old-fashioned. :)

Well, in fact, societies have been dealing with such questions, who culturally accept such differentiation, what remains to be seen is whether the human condition will become so that we use "immutable" science to justify segregation, much like the past, and with eugenics.

Create the perfect baby, this already happens in the Netherlands, where 95% of foetuses with indicators of Down Syndrome are aborted. However, I do support gene editing to remove harmful diseases, like in China, even though he was removed. Even so, maybe I shouldn't, since who knows where such a system would stop?

Better to deal with one's difficulties than to seek a solution which can be misused. The answer to all technological process.

Program, de-program, expand, contract, engineer, de-engineer humanity and the human condition, the world has much foolishness, and it'll likely continue into the future anyways.

Or perhaps we will conserve them, as we hunt them, endangered species, or in zoos, or perhaps we will coexist and intermingle like the Neanderthals and Homo Sapiens as oft repeated, one could say history repeats itself while it also simultaneously branches off into other directions.

The Malmstrom Effect

How one of the most well-documented UFO cases has been forgotten

Unrecognizable Person Observing Red and Blue Lights on Road at Night by Slava MKRVSKY on pexels.com

Addendum: The Draft Article is up on EverybodyWiki:

https://en.everybodywiki.com/Malmstrom_Air_Force_Base_UFO_incident

Author's Note: This note is so long, as it is required to give proper context for this writing work. If this article seems to be haphazard and incoherent, it is because it was made for Wikipedia and I'm transposing it here.

Compared to other topics, the level of scrutiny on the UFO issue is particularly hostile and neurotic, one would think that it was as if Wikipedians who are in charge of everything by virtue of their time spent and editing prowess and bureaucratic intimidation, it was as if they would rather have UFOs not exist. It is true that I had put this up as a draft article on Wikipedia to be published, it was on the Dispute Resolution's Moderator's personal Wikipedia "Draft Article" page, I had hoped that someone else would take it up and do it, perhaps the moderator or someone else, but I had left and the six month period had got over and it got deleted, however, what did I expect in all honesty? Still, while I'm almost certainly sure that there was no malice, just ignorance, disinterest or the work on thousands of other articles, I do wonder whether the giggle factor, or the bureaucratic intimidation on Wikipedia, prevented anyone to write or expand or publish it as their own?

One of the most striking examples of this I have seen, is Youtube videos linked as sources on other articles of some note, I don't remember them clearly now, and sourced government documents being scoffed at in Wikipedia. Which is a strange doublethink as well, as there is undue weight and deference given to UFO-related government documents on Wikipedia, when the government is well-known to obfuscate the truth, one need only look at the documents destroyed by the US government related to Project MKULTRA, how can you have freedom of information, if there is no information?

My Wikipedia ID is or was "Chantern15", you can see this absurdity in action, when you go to the archives of the reliable sources page. The Blackvault.com, which has studiously collected millions of pages of government documents, is dismissed as an unreliable source, as one editor said that all the documents there were faked by the site owner (John Greenewald Jr.). 2 million+ pages over 32–33 years, is the ludicrous amount of roughly 60–62.5 thousand pages a year or 164 + pages a day. Even if we say that most of the documents are frivolous and of poor quality, Maria Lopez who wrote 4,000 books over her lifetime, and let's be generous and say that each novel had 300 pages, that's roughly 1.2 million pages over a lifetime! I suppose we are to believe that John Greenewald is 3.34 times more prolific than the author who wrote the most novels!

Let me add further to this absurdity, before I start the article so that you understand what I mean, you must be wondering, if you are a Wikipedia editor, why I didn't take up dispute resolution, it's a time-consuming process, and I wanted to save it for something that I had enough evidence to back up in creating an article. I started the Dispute Resolution for adding the Malmstrom UFO base incident on the US UFO sightings page. As I was blocked by what seems to be two perennial UFO editors who seem to collaborate with each other to maintain a hard-skeptic, borderline denialist stance on UFOs. To be fair to them, they seem atleast somewhat open to conversation, but that should not be the bar that we aim for. My additions to the Identification Studies of UFOs had little or no qualms, or if they did, they found their own sources to add my points, even if in their voice, so to speak, as much as their voice, either through omission or restructuring they can get past the Wikipedia NPOV.

One is not going to dispute everything, because quickly you'll find that Wikipedia is a full-time unpaid job, 12 hours a day and so on, if you're fully dedicated. The bias on Wikipedia maybe to the Left, but it's also towards those who can afford with time or money to sit through the whole day and scan the articles they like to edit. And I mean even more so than the person who sits 12 hours a day to edit or dispute.

Anyways, my dispute had many sources, 14 or more, now the sources can be disputed, which I present, I have no problem. I wanted a very long explanation, like 5 + paragraphs, some UFO enteries on that summary, are a big paragraph, that's cool, I'm happy even if I get that. Plus, the party I have raised the dispute against doesn't have to be present during the Dispute Resolution, however I ask the resolver to include them, as they had been absent for sometime, we agree on a short 2–4 line entry, with only a single year entry, no other date data, these events are also multi-year and no other geographical location besides Malmstrom, and while unsatisfactory and I realize in my mind, not perfectly NPOV, I agree, better to have something than nothing, mind you, I had government documents through John's FOIA on hand, but even so, even if it is rejected as unreliable, maybe those documents exist on a third party website too, it's possible, this would still bring up questions of reliability and credibility, anyways that short para is there and the resolver or moderator rules that without an article, no other UFO entry will be included on the summary page, I leave Wikipedia shortly after this.

Curiosity takes the better of me, and a few months later I visit that page for the 4th or 5th time, and that entry is gone! It's removal is not even present on the history page, God knows why?! And as for that no-summary-entry-in-US-UFO-incidents-without-a-dedicated-article-rule, I saw a few entries with no dedicated articles, seemingly properly sourced (and unsourced), but how neutral, I don't know.

There's a bit more to this story and there are other things that I can tell you about, but I don't want to take up more space than needed, perhaps we could have a private conversation, or you can just take a look at my post history on my retired Wikipedia editor page and the DR and RS archives by searching my editor ID.

Here's the Malmstrom UFO story as best as I can source it, cleaned up to look a bit prettier, stripped a bit of its Wikipedia format, but mostly left unmolested (sources and further reading to be at the bottom). I don't claim that all my sources are the best or free of bias, however, it is good that as many perspectives as can be included can be. It's hard to imagine self-proclaimed "Libertarians" in the US style can create a website that becomes captured by "Anarchists" who are ardent bureaucrats from the bottom up, it's very reminiscent of how the anarchist society on the planet Anarres in the Hainish Cycle book, "The Dispossessed" devolves into, to seek inspiration from Trotsky's words, "A degenerated bureaucratic worker's society", with a paramountcy of rules, and doing things as always before, I think that quite succinctly sums up what has happened to Wikipedia. It's an authoritarian anarchic bureaucracy, with the one who wields the biggest stick, here the stick being time and bureaucratic intimidation, wins and dominates the rest, the "No Rules" Rule be damned, this shows that authoritarianism can be as much as from below as from above, especially in a cyber system, where dissent can be more easily marginalized than the physical world.

I can't tell you what those objects were or where they came from, they certainly acted strangely and had highly advanced capabilities, characteristics which are often associated by some laymen and a few experts with extraterrestrial or interdimensional life, humans from the future, advanced tech on Earth, experimental in nature, some transcendent thought being or beings trying to interact, test or play with us and many other exotic or mundane descriptions, from hallucinations, mirages, mass hysteria, temperature inversions, spoofing, etc., etc. although how a spoof or false flag operation, or a mirage, mass hysteria or any other such myriad of explanations can explain RADAR-Visual sightings with multiple witnesses and the effect on its surroundings, I'll be buggered to know. The writer of the 2022 book Anomaly, Daniel Coumbe, attempting a scientific analysis of the best cases with good data and significance, came to the conclusion in his book that the best unexplained cases of UFOs are non-manmade, non-natural physical phenomena. Which then makes us ask the skeptics, if it's not man-made, not natural, not from here (advanced tech), not from there (supernatural beings, aliens, interdimensional or interuniversal beings, etc. etc.), they are physical (they interact with the material world as you and I do, even if for us, they do so strangely), then it begs the question, what are they? If they're real but not anything, it creates a paradox. Maybe it's like the Monty Python Argument Clinic Sketch, they're coming here in their spare time! :D

Hopefully this article contains a sufficient number of different viewpoints to be satisfactory as a jumping off point.

Article Begins —

What's That In The Sky?

A report of an Unidentified Flying Object at Malmstrom Air Force Base on March 16, 1967, involved reports of unidentified aircraft that allegedly affected the operational status of missile systems at the base.

Rtd. Captain Robert Salas, a nuclear launch control officer at Malmstrom Air Force Base had his statement about UFOs interfering with nuclear missiles at Malmstrom (the 10 missiles, called a flight, went off alert status) covered in many news outlets which mirrored his statements in a National Press Club meeting in 2010, which Stephanie Mercier writing for Vice points out that critics noticed that each of the committee members were being paid $20,000 and all expenses paid for their participation in the hearing (but it's common for speakers to be given some recompensation, however whether this is normal recompense or outsize, I'll leave my American viewers to decide).

Leslie Kean writes that on the morning of the 24th of March 1967, then first lieutenant Robert Salas, the air force's nuclear launch control officer stationed at the base for Oscar flight received a call from a frightened security guard who reported that a UFO flying directly over the

Oscar Flight Control Center at the base...Salas immediately woke up the first crew commander, First Lieutenant Fred Meiwald...then within minutes of the call, the missiles started to shut down, one by one. Salas said that "they went into no-go while the ufo were overhead...this means that they were disabled, not launchable".

A week earlier, on the morning of March 9, 1967, 35 miles (56 kms) from Oscar Flight, UFOs had visited the echo flight facility and all of its missiles went down too. A declassified document, dated March '67, but after the 17th, from Strategic Air Command contains a telex, with the subject heading, "Loss of strategic alert, echo flight, malmstrom afb". It further reads, "All ten missiles in echo flight at Malmstrom lost strat alert within ten seconds of each other. This incident occurred at 6845L on 16th March 1967. As of this date, all missiles have been returned to strat". The document further includes the statement, "grave concern to this headquarters", emphasizes the need for "in-depth analysis to determine cause and corrective action" and highlights the "urgency of this problem" and guarantees "full cooperation and support".

The Airforce Launches An Investigation

An analysis into this incident which happened at echo flight was forthcoming as documents revealed through a Freedom of Information Act request at the website, "The Black Vault". The documents describe the investigation as, "On 16th March 1967 at 0845, all sites in Echo (E) Flight, Malmstrom AFB, shutdown with no-go indication of channels 9 and 12 on Voice Reporting Signal Assemble (VRSA)". Analysis of channel 50 data from E-7 and E-8 revealed that both sites were shutdown as a result of external influence to the G&C (guidance and control), no no-gos were detected by the G&C. A no-go cause of shutdown for the flight would've reflected in channel 50 data. The non-detectable from the G&C which could've caused a shutdown would've been the loss of confirm codes. An investigation of the logic coupler lead to the conclusion that the possibility of external generated signals causing this shutdown would've been very remote, as all 10 couplers would have to fail within seconds of each other. And so would've a partial reset of all. Investigations into the cause of the event covered cable connections in the Electric Surge Arrestor (ESA) room, the logic coupler, electric failure at the substation, the transformers, the presence of Boeing Company teams (who came after the incident), commercial power, poor switching, microsecond pulses of square waves in the Sensitive Information Network (SIN) lines, EMP testing in the SIN and Sensitive Command Network (SCN), transformer failure in the stock watering area, the interconnecting box, arcing, burnt areas, tampering and adverse power/electrical effects led to either a negative result or were considered highly remote. Tests also took place at Warren AFB and "D" flight. Rumors of UFOs around the time of the fault were disproven (through questioning air traffic controllers and reviewing RADAR data). A similar incident occurred at Alpha flight in the December of 1966. Echo flight had had issues with electric systems prior to this incident.

After the investigations were concluded, upgrades called "Force Mod EMP modification" took place, many which were the addition of major sub-assembly containing zener diodes, isolation transformers and common-mode transformers for each SIN/SCN pair. Modifications independent of these were to the cable assembly set, by revising the wiring to VRSA channels 26 and 27 and replacing all the batteries by the 14th of October (1967). Further EMP/Electrostatic testing was mentioned and conducted. The investigation documentation concludes with, *****the investigation of the incident could not discover the cause of the incident, but it was believed to be a freak incident*****.

The Speculation Begins

Robert Hastings observes that "the Air Force remains entirely silent on the Oscar Flight shutdown, which apparently occurred a few days later" (later or earlier? The document mentions it happened a weak before Echo Flight, maybe Robert Hastings got his dates mixed up, the more suspicious of you might see this as some kind of inconsistency, but I'll leave that to you).

Scott Mansch interviewed Robert Salas for the Great Falls Tribune, where he (Robert Salas) states that "I think this was a message, just a message. Because they did not damage the equipment. It wasn't like they destroyed the weapons. It was just a weapon. I believe we have got to get rid of nuclear weapons because they're so dangerous."

Benjamin Radford writing for Live Science, points out that, "if extraterrestrial intelligences have been watching over humanity and are so concerned about nuclear weapons, why didn't they prevent the atomic bombings of Hiroshima and Nagasaki at the end of World War II?" (Unless I am mistaken, this seems like the Straw Man logical fallacy, i.e. if the aliens disabled Malmstrom's missiles, why didn't they disable the bombs meant for Hiroshima and Nagasaki? Of course, this, my observation, can't be included in the article, because as far as I know there is no response to this comment, but I wish Ben Radford had come up with a better argument, because I have read his book on scientific skepticism).

(I will need assistance in shortening this part below from "Ward Sinclair...spotted the object", as I'm unsure of how to keep the meaning of the article intact while keeping it concise)

Ward Sinclair and Art Harris writing for the Washington Post describe an incident which took place at Malmstrom Air Force Base on the 7th of November 1975, where an off-duty missile launch officer, by the name of Captain Thomas W. O'brien stated that an

aircraft *****resembling***** a helicopter approached the silo area. He and an unnamed deputy were resting in a building when they heard what they *****thought***** was a helicopter rotor. The deputy looked out the window and saw what he described as "the silhouette of a large aircraft hovering about 10 to 15 feet above the ground" and about 25 feet from the launch-area fence.

He reportedly saw two red and white lights on the front, a white light on the bottom and another on the rear. Darkness prevented him from seeing markings or personnel on the object. The object left after a minute or so of hovering, the report said.

Military crews at two other nearby launch facilities reported moving lights in the air on the same evening, but said they heard no sounds.

NORAD commanders' activity logs during that period of time reported another sighting at another unidentified launch facility in which witnesses said they saw the object "issuing a black object from, it, tubular in shape." Standard radar surveillance provided no clues as to the presence of anything other than known craft in the area.

More detail appeared in reports of sightings on Oct. 30 and 31 over Wurtsmith AFB, where an "unidentified helicopter" flew around the base and hovered over weapons-storage bunkers.

Investigators subsequently determined that *****no military, commercial or private helicopters known to be based in the area could have been around Wurtsmith at those times*****. The crew of a KC135 tanker plane, already airborne, spotted the object near the base and attempted to give chase, but couldn't keep up with it.

Several sightings occurred at the Maine air base as well, where objects hovered over the weapons area. Radar and visual sightings were made, and another KC135 was sent aloft to oversee pursuit efforts by a helicopter borrowed from the Maine National Guard — Loring had none of its own.

The object eventually disappeared toward the Canadian border, where Canadian air force jets were on alert. There was no indication whether the Canadian planes spotted the object.

Inconclusive But Strange

Jacqueline Alemany interviewing Luis Elizondo, the former director of the now defunct AATIP (alleged by US investigative journalist Steven Greenstreet for the New York Post in his Youtube Series on the UFO phenomenon

"The Basement Office" to be a former unofficial and unfunded project in the Pentagon which dealt with more than just UFOs, including supposed paranormal activities and entities, with Louis Elizondo as its former unofficial head), in a response to her question about luring UFOs/UAPs through nuclear powered aircraft carriers, mentions as a part of his answer that, "Now in this country we've had incidents where these UAPs have interfered and actually brought offline our nuclear capabilities. And I think to some they would probably say, well, that's a sign that whatever this is, is something that is peaceful. But in the same context, we also have data suggesting that in other countries these things have interfered with their nuclear technology and actually turned them on, put them online".

Additionally, with reference to Post-Project Blue Book U.S.A.F U.F.O activities, Howard Blum reports that that Freedom of Information Act requests show that the U.S. Air Force has continued to catalog and track UFO sightings, particularly a series of dozens of UFO encounters from the late 1960s to the mid-1970s that occurred at U.S. military facilities with nuclear weapons. Blum writes that some of these official documents depart drastically from the normally dry and bureaucratic wording of government paperwork, making obvious the sense of "terror" that these UFO incidents inspired in many U.S.A.F. personnel.

Philip.J.Klass writing for the LA Times, observes in a review of the book from which the above excerpt has been taken, that it has many factual errors, including with reference to claims about him.

[Now Deceased Physicist Stanton Friedman, an advocate for UFOs and further research in them, was critical of Philip, and said that he (Philip) lost a bet with him on the subject of UFOs and their evidence, if memory serves correctly. That is Friedman could produce documents and establish the teletypers at that time were of the make and model used frequently by the airforce at the time, but viewing the source that I have included below should give a better idea to y'all].

The Armour of God

As you can see, the UFO issue has become seemingly impenetrable like the aforementioned Armour of God, in this field of study, fragmented data which needs to be collated from various different sources each with competing interpretations and views of the phenomena, and while some studies from Kevin H Knuth and the current outgoing president of AARO (The All- Domain Anomaly Resolution Office), Dr. Sean Kirkpatrick, show that while UAP could have speeds compliant with interstellar travel (Kevin H Knuth) or that they could be self-replicating seeds (probes) dropped from larger motherships speeding through our solar system (like some interstellar comets or comet-mimics or anything else, better known as interstellar objects), as proposed by Dr. Kirkpatrick, or something more mundane and Earthly that we missed (and this would allow us to recalibrate our equipments and techniques) the nature of the phenomenon leads oftentimes to fragmented, contradictory and fleeting data, not to mention the human element which complicates all these ingredients, it requires a multi-disciplinary approach, historical analysis and neutrality.

All of which are being worked towards, however, in my view the phenomenon is such, for those few cases, where we have information beyond a shadow of doubt that this is real but strange, I know a few things, it is an intelligent system carrying out a function and it requires repeatability and involves the study of humans, or some sort of natural or artificial automata that brilliantly mimics these behaviours but is mundane, both of which would be fascinating. Who or what is using them is unknown to me, due to the surprisingly varied nature of the phenomenon. Perhaps Malmstrom and its related airbases have been forgotten not only because of the secrecy of the Cold War, or undermining US supremacy, but also likely due to the profound realization that it isn't just about a blip on a RADAR or a blur in the air, but the potential for physical interaction on such a sensitive scale as nuclear weapons, which demands a closer look, even if only because National Security compels such a deep look. Even the ardent denialist would be challenged to see closer as a breach at a nuclear missile silo cannot be ignored, as if the hand of God itself commanded our attention from the heavens. Furthermore, each appearance properly studied and each effect properly measured leads us, all of us, inexorably, inevitably to the truth.

Sources

1. Former Airmen to Govt.: Come Clean on UFOs — ABC News

2. The truth about UFOs is out there, and US students are trying to find it | US education | The Guardian

3. 'Project Blue Book' Is Based on a True U.F.O. Story. Here It Is. — The New York Times (archive.org)

4. UFOs in America: A short history of aliens and sightings — CNN

5. Aliens land ... in the headlines (nbcnews.com)

6. Tinfoil Tuesdays: UFOs Neutered Nukes, Officers Claim | WIRED

7. Ex-Air Force Personnel: UFOs Deactivated Nukes — CBS News

8. AM — Aliens are watching nukes, according to retired officers 28/09/2010 (abc.net.au)

9. Air Force officers recount ridicule after sharing UFO experiences — Washington Times

10. 10.UFO conspiracy hearing boosted by former congressmen and senator | UFOs | The Guardian

11. 11.A Bunch of Alien Lovers Held a Fake Congressional Hearing about Aliens. What Now? (vice.com)

12. Kean, Leslie, UFOs: Generals, Pilots and Government Officials Go On The Record, Crown Publishing, 2010, pg 144

13. UFOsMalmstromAFB_SACmessageMarch16th1967 .jpg (698×936) (earthfiles.com)

14. 14.341st Strategic Missile Wing History Excerpts, 1 Jan Mar 67–31 Mar 68, 84 pages,

Fifteenth Air Force, Strategic Air Command, Declassified between 27 Apr 95 and 27 Jul 95, Pg 32, 33, 36, 37, 38, 39, P31, P32, P33, P63, Pg65, Pg66, Pg67, PG68, PG68+1, +2,

Pg57, 60, malmstromufo.pdf (theblackvault.com) (Don't blame me for the numbering system, that's the disorganized and inchronological state they were found in, post-FOIA request)

15. Hastings, Robert, UFOs and Nukes Extraordinary Encounters at Nuclear Weapons Sites, Second Edition, 2017, Ch 11, 4th para

16. https://www.greatfallstribune.com/story/news/2017/02/26/mansch-montana-ufo-sighting-stillresonates/98452858/

17. Did UFOs Disarm Nuclear Weapons? And If So, Why? | Live Science

18. What Were Those Mysterious Craft? — The Washington Post

19. https://www.washingtonpost.com/people/jacqueline-alemany

20. Transcript: UFOs & National Security with Luis Elizondo, Former Director, Advanced Aerospace Threat Identification Program — The Washington Post

21. Blum, Howard, Out There: The Government's Secret Quest for Extraterrestrials, Simon and Schuster, 1990

22. https://www.latimes.com/archives/la-xpm-1990-09-02-bk-1953-story.html

Further Reading/Viewing

1. Enigma Labs has a great article on this very topic, with some information that I inadvertantly missed, I hope that it is useful to you (if it goes offline, enter the link on archive.org). https://enigmalabs.io/library/dd644338-b5d7-45a8-995a-b72fa4be68d1

2. Steven Greenstreet's coverage on the doubtful AATIP: https://youtu.be/6XD4gQS_-qY?t=2071&si=1UUDVMIGTYlmD9aG

3. Stanton Friedman's criticism of Philip J Klass, the second video is a discussion between them, you can find more by searching on Dr. Friedman: https://www.youtube.com/watch?v=7OiOpxGj-QI https://www.youtube.com/watch?v=AW6xj9xCs_8

4. Coumbe, Daniel, Anomaly, 2022 (can be purchased on Amazon.com, not a sponsorship)

5. Vallée, Jacques, Passport To Magonia, 1969

6. Hynek, J. Allen, The UFO Experience, 1972

7. Ruppelt, Edward J., The Report On Unidentified Flying Objects, 1956

8. Radford, Benjamin, Scientific Paranormal Investigation, 2010

9. Estimating Flight Characteristics of Anomalous Unidentified

Aerial Vehicles; Knuth, Kevin H. Powell, Robert M., Reali, Peter A., University at Albany, State University of New York, Physics Faculty, 2019.

10. PHYSICAL CONSTRAINTS ON UNIDENTIFIED AERIAL PHENOMENA; Loeb,

Abraham (Avi), Kirkpatrick, Dr. Sean, University of Harvard, Astronomy Department and The All-Domain Anomaly Resolution Office, 2023.

11. https://www.cufon.org/cufon/malmstrom/malm1.htm

Why I Am A Conservative Socialist

A Just Society Requires Both Ordered Liberty And Social Ownership Of The Means Of Production And Profit With Sanctity For Life

Opinion Piece

If ideology is fallible and self-contradictory, then what is it that one can believe?

In my view, the least contradictory ideology is Conservative Socialism, and I'll tell you why.

Like Classical Conservatism, Conservatism in Socialism, is the Social aspect, and it is also a statement against rapid and aggressive progress.

Humans are irrational and unpredictable and self-destructive.

Criticisms of those which exaggerate these qualities, such as Liberalism and unrestricted Capitalism, allow for these excesses to fester, lead to their own demise by allowing a culture of unbidden hedonism and egocentrism to take hold, which cannot allow for proper future planning, allow for sustained population sizes over the span of 1000+ years or any other such behaviour which allows complex society to exist over long timescales. It is a historical aberration. Conservatism recognizes that ordered Liberty requires religion, the state, social cohesion and belonging and a sense of transcendental purpose and the value of life and to stand against the concentration of power and wealth and soul-crushing poverty and the alienation and dehumanization of rote work, as Edmund Burke observed, to prevent centrifugal forces from spinning society apart.

Socialism, in its worker-run form, with Market Socialism and Ethics ensures a good distribution of wealth and profits in society, with the denouement of transactionalism which has permeated all of modern society and in every sphere. A man who cannot look after himself cannot be free under overbureaucratic, lumbering state and the machinations of corporations.

With market socialism, workers can trade their goods and services for currency, spread the proceedings, feel like they have meaning in their lives, carry out meaningful work and not be beholden to state power through welfare or corporate power through the punishment of starvation or death, if they do not work for capitalists.

In a conservative socialist society, where life is protected, workers are respected, power is distributed equitably, culture is preserved, distributed and expanded freely, socialism is adopted ethically and wealth is distributed broadly, where Materialism, Capitalist, Socialist or Philosophical or Scientific takes a backseat to spiritual, artistic, humanistic progress, this will foster a newfound sense of human association and freedom, freedom in its old-fashioned sense, where the individual was embedded into a greater collective whole, fostering the spirit of a united personhood, where the rights of the individual were protected not just by the individual but also by society, with a sense of mutual obligation, lacking in aggressively capitalist, authoritarian and individualist societies, or their counterparts in socialism.

Divorcing fanatical materialism from Socialism is important to avoid the pitfalls present in Capitalist materialism too. Humans cannot and should not be treated as mainly rational economic agents, from a capitalist or a socialist perspective, they should be treated as spiritual and communal (communal in its pro-community sense, not the casteist or divisive sense) beings first and foremost, then and only then can a just and moral society exist without tyranny or exploitation.

Further Reading:

1. https://quillette.com/2022/12/27/on-conservative-socialism/

www.ingramcontent.com/pod-product-compliance
Lightning Source LLC
LaVergne TN
LVHW061613070526
838199LV00078B/7261